fine Cooking
Roasting

fine Cooking
Roasting

Editors and contributors of *Fine Cooking*

The Taunton Press

Front cover recipe: Spice-Rubbed Roast Beef Tenderloin, p. 82

The Taunton Press
Inspiration for hands-on living®

The Taunton Press, Inc.
63 South Main Street
PO Box 5506, Newtown, CT 06470-5506
email: tp@taunton.com

Editor: Carolyn Mandarano
Copy editor: Nina Rynd Whitnah
Indexer: Heidi Blough
Jacket/Cover design: Kimberly Adis
Cover photographer: Hector Sanchez
Interior photographer: Scott Phillips © The Taunton Press, Inc., except the following: p. 6: © Quentin Bacon; pp. 66-67: © Hector Sanchez; pp. 106-107: © Tukka Koshi; p. 123 (bottom): Ruth Lively © The Taunton Press, Inc.; pp. 124-126: © Colin Clark

Fine Cooking® is a trademark of The Taunton Press, Inc., registered in the U.S. Patent and Trademark Office.

The following names/manufacturers appearing in *Fine Cooking Roasting* are trademarks:
Budweiser®, Business Elite®, Colman's®, Diamond Crystal®, Fage®, Grand Marnier®,
Morton®, Newcastle®, Pyrex®

Library of Congress Cataloging-in-Publication Data

Fine cooking roasting : favorite recipes & essential tips for chicken, beef, veggies & more / editors of Fine cooking.
     pages cm
  Includes index.
  ISBN 978-1-62710-807-2
  1. Roasting (Cooking) I. Taunton's fine cooking. II. Title: Roasting.
  TX690.F565 2014
  641.7'1--dc23
                    2014024594

Printed in the United States of America
10 9 8 7 6 5 4 3 2

Slow-Roasted Pork
Shoulder with Carrots,
Onions, and Garlic, p. 102

Oven Ready

IF YOU'RE LIKE MANY OF US, you're ready to crank up the oven as soon
as the temperature dips into sweatshirt territory. That's why this book
celebrates roasting, a method that's simple, largely hands-off, and brings
out bold, intense flavor in foods, from beef and fish to fruits and vegetables.
Throughout the book, you'll find a wide range of recipes, from the
caramelized, butternut squash main-dish salad on p. 9, to the rich roast
beef with red-wine sauce on p. 82, to a fabulous dry-brined turkey on p. 57.
In addition to the beef and turkey above, there are a host of recipes that are
holiday feast-worthy, such as the Tuscan-Style Roast Pork with Rosemary,
Sage, and Garlic on p. 94 and also quick, easy weeknight meals, like the
Garlicky Shrimp with Basil on p. 32. In all, more than 90 great recipes to
keep your oven on all season long.

—The *Fine Cooking* Editors

contents

Sweet Potato, Ham, and
Goat Cheese Salad, p. 7

Soups & Salads

Roasted vegetables add deep flavor and contrasting textures to these dishes.

the recipes

For best browning, don't overcrowd the baking sheet.

roasted potato and mushroom salad with mascarpone

Roasting the potatoes and mushrooms deepens the flavor of this warm salad, and the mascarpone dressing adds richness and tang.

Serves 6 to 8

- 6 Tbs. extra-virgin olive oil
- 2 lb. Yukon Gold potatoes (about 6 medium), scrubbed, halved, and cut into ¾-inch wedges

  Kosher salt and freshly ground black pepper
- ¾ lb. small to medium cremini or white mushrooms, quartered
- ½ cup mascarpone
- ¼ cup fresh orange juice
- 1½ tsp. red-wine vinegar
- ⅓ cup thinly sliced scallions (white and green parts; about 4 small)

Position a rack in the center of the oven and heat the oven to 450°F. Coat a large rimmed baking sheet with 1 Tbs. of the oil.

In a large bowl, toss the potatoes, 2 Tbs. of the oil, 1 tsp. salt, and ½ tsp. pepper. Arrange in a single layer on the prepared baking sheet. Roast until barely tender, about 20 minutes, gently tossing with a spatula halfway through.

Meanwhile, toss the mushrooms, 1 Tbs. of the oil, ½ tsp. salt, and ¼ tsp. pepper in the bowl.

Gently toss the potatoes again, scatter the mushrooms evenly over the potatoes, and continue to roast until both the potatoes and mushrooms are tender and golden-brown in spots, another 10 to 15 minutes.

Meanwhile, in a medium bowl, whisk the mascarpone, orange juice, vinegar, 1 tsp. salt, and ⅛ tsp. pepper. Drizzle in the remaining 2 Tbs. oil while whisking constantly; set aside.

Return the potatoes and mushrooms to the large bowl and add the mascarpone dressing. Toss gently to coat, season to taste with salt and pepper, and transfer to a large serving bowl. Garnish with the scallions and serve.

roasted hubbard squash soup with hazelnuts and chives

If you can't find Espelette pepper, use just a pinch of cayenne instead. The soup keeps for 3 days in the refrigerator or for 2 months in the freezer.

Yields about 10 cups; serves 8 to 10

3	Tbs. extra-virgin olive oil
3	large cloves garlic, peeled
1	Tbs. coriander seeds
1½	tsp. fennel seeds
1½	tsp. dried sage
1	small (5½- to 6-lb.) hubbard squash, halved lengthwise and seeded (see p. 127)
2	Tbs. unsalted butter
1	large leek (white and light-green parts only), halved lengthwise and thinly sliced crosswise
2	medium carrots, peeled and cut into small dice
	Kosher salt
5	cups homemade or lower-salt chicken or vegetable broth
1	bay leaf
2	tsp. fresh lemon juice
	Freshly ground black pepper
½	cup hazelnuts, toasted, skinned, and chopped
2	Tbs. thinly sliced fresh chives
	Several small pinches of Espelette pepper or cayenne

Position a rack in the center of the oven and heat the oven to 400°F. Line a heavy-duty rimmed baking sheet with parchment.

In a mortar and pestle, pound the oil, garlic, coriander seeds, fennel seeds, and sage until they resemble a coarse paste. Rub the spice mixture on the flesh of the squash halves. Set them cut side down on the prepared pan and roast until tender when pierced with a fork, about 1 hour.

Let cool, cut side up. When cool enough to handle, scrape the flesh away from the rind—you'll need about 5 cups.

Melt the butter in a 5- to 6-quart Dutch oven over medium heat. Add the leek, carrots, and a big pinch of salt and cook, stirring occasionally, until the leek is softened, 8 to 10 minutes. Add the squash, broth, bay leaf, and 1 tsp. salt and bring to a boil over high heat. Reduce the heat to a low simmer, cover, and cook for 30 minutes to develop the soup's flavor.

Remove the bay leaf and allow the soup to cool slightly. Purée the soup in batches in a blender. Return the soup to the pot and add the lemon juice. Season to taste with salt and pepper. Garnish with the chopped hazelnuts, chives, and Espelette pepper or cayenne.

cucumber, fennel, and roasted potato salad with parsleyed yogurt

This refreshing, almost palate-cleansing side dish is served with a dollop of cool, creamy yogurt. It pairs perfectly with lamb. **Serves 6 to 8**

- 1½ lb. fingerling potatoes
- ¼ cup extra-virgin olive oil; more to taste

   Kosher salt and freshly ground black pepper
- ½ lb. haricots verts or slender green beans, trimmed
- 1½ cups plain whole-milk Greek yogurt, such as Fage® Total
- 1½ Tbs. chopped fresh flat-leaf parsley
- 3 medium ribs celery, trimmed and sliced ⅛ inch thick on a sharp diagonal
- 1 English cucumber, peeled, cut in half lengthwise, seeded, and sliced ⅛ inch thick on the diagonal

- 1 medium bulb fennel (about 1 lb.), trimmed, cut in half, cored, and sliced crosswise ⅛ inch thick
- 1 small red onion, halved and sliced crosswise ⅛ inch thick
- 1 Tbs. fresh lemon juice; more to taste

Position a rack in the center of the oven and heat the oven to 400°F. On a small rimmed baking sheet, toss the potatoes with 1 Tbs. of the oil and season generously with salt and pepper. Roast until tender when pierced with a skewer, 25 to 30 minutes. Cool the potatoes; they can be served still warm or at room temperature.

Meanwhile, bring a medium saucepan of salted water to a boil. Cook the haricots verts until just tender (taste one to see), 3 to 4 minutes. Drain in a colander and run under cold water until cool.

Combine the yogurt and parsley and season well with salt and pepper; keep chilled until ready to serve.

To serve, halve or quarter any larger fingerlings but leave the tiny ones whole. Combine the potatoes, haricots verts, celery, cucumber, fennel, and red onion in a large bowl and toss with the remaining 3 Tbs. oil and the lemon juice. Season well with salt and pepper and toss again. Taste and add more lemon juice or olive oil if needed. Portion the salad into 6 to 8 servings. Add a large dollop of yogurt to each salad.

sweet potato, ham, and goat cheese salad

Look for high-quality, all-natural ham steak for the best flavor and texture.
Serves 4

- 1 medium yellow onion, halved lengthwise and cut into ½-inch wedges
- 1 medium sweet potato, peeled and cut into ¼-inch rounds
- ½ cup extra-virgin olive oil
- 1¼ tsp. chopped fresh rosemary
  Kosher salt and freshly ground black pepper
- ¾ lb. ham steak (preferably "ham with natural juices"), cut into ¾-inch cubes (2 cups)
- 2 Tbs. pure maple syrup
- 2 Tbs. balsamic vinegar
- 5 oz. mesclun salad mix
- 4 oz. fresh goat cheese, crumbled

Position a rack in the center of the oven and heat the oven to 450°F. Line a rimmed baking sheet with foil. On the baking sheet, toss the onion, sweet potato, 2 Tbs. of the oil, 1 tsp. of the rosemary, ½ tsp. salt, and ¼ tsp. pepper and spread in a single layer. Roast until the vegetables start to become tender, about 15 minutes.

In a small bowl, toss the ham with the maple syrup. Push the vegetables on the baking sheet aside to make room for the ham and bake until the ham and onions are browned in places, about 10 minutes.

Meanwhile, in a small bowl, whisk the remaining 6 Tbs. oil with the vinegar, the remaining ¼ tsp. rosemary, and ¼ tsp. each salt and pepper. In a large bowl, toss the mesclun with ¼ cup of the vinaigrette. Season to taste with salt and pepper.

Divide the mesclun among 4 plates. Top with the roasted vegetables and ham. Sprinkle each salad with some of the goat cheese. Drizzle with the remaining vinaigrette and serve.

southwest tomato and roasted pepper soup

Roasted red peppers add just the right amount of sweetness to this rich and silky tomato soup. **Yields about 5¾ cups; serves 5 to 6**

- 1 large red bell pepper
- 3 Tbs. plus ½ tsp. extra-virgin olive oil
- 1 large yellow onion, finely chopped
- 1 tsp. chili powder
- 1 tsp. ground cumin
- ¼ tsp. ground coriander
- 3 cups lower-salt chicken broth
- 1 28-oz. can whole peeled plum tomatoes, drained and coarsely chopped (reserve the juice)
- 1 cup small-diced zucchini
- ½ cup sour cream
- 1 Tbs. lime juice
- ½ tsp. finely grated lime zest
  Kosher salt and freshly ground pepper
- 2 Tbs. loosely packed fresh cilantro leaves

Coat the pepper with ½ tsp. of the oil. Roast directly on the grate of a gas burner over high heat or under a broiler, turning the pepper occasionally until charred all over. Put the pepper in a bowl while still hot and cover the bowl with plastic wrap. Let rest until cool enough to handle. Stem, seed, and peel the pepper, using a table knife to scrape away the charred skin. Coarsely chop the pepper and set aside.

In a nonreactive 5- to 6-quart Dutch oven, heat the remaining 3 Tbs. oil over medium-low heat. Add the onion and cook, stirring occasionally, until just soft, 8 to 10 minutes. Stir the chili powder, cumin, and coriander into the onions. Add the roasted pepper and cook for another minute. Add the broth and tomatoes and bring to a simmer over medium-high heat. Reduce the heat to low, cover, and simmer for 40 minutes.

Let cool briefly and then purée the soup in two or three batches in a blender or food processor. Rinse the pot and return the soup to the pot. If it is too thick, add some of the reserved tomato juice.

Add the zucchini and cook for another 10 minutes over low heat.

Meanwhile, combine the sour cream, lime juice, and lime zest in a small bowl. Season the soup to taste with salt and pepper. Serve garnished with the lime sour cream and the cilantro leaves.

Make Ahead

The soup can be made up to 3 days ahead and refrigerated. Garnish with the sorghum butter and cracklings just before serving.

roasted sweet potato soup with sorghum butter and duck cracklings

This is a rich dish with a terrific crispy duck skin and nutty butter garnish on top. Duck cracklings are made from the leftover skin after dressing a duck. Ask your butcher if he will sell you just the skin, or buy a duck or duck breasts and save the meat for another use. Alternatively, you can substitute crisped pancetta for the cracklings.

Serves 6

FOR THE SOUP

- 4 medium sweet potatoes (about 2 lb. total)
- 2 Tbs. unsalted butter
- 2 Tbs. olive oil
- 1 small yellow onion, finely chopped (¾ cup)
- 1 quart lower-salt chicken broth
  Kosher salt
- ¾ cup heavy cream
- ¼ cup buttermilk

FOR THE DUCK CRACKLINGS

- 1 lb. duck skin (from 1 medium duck or 4 duck breasts)
- 1 bay leaf
  Kosher salt

FOR THE SORGHUM BROWN BUTTER

- 4 Tbs. unsalted butter, cut into cubes
- 2 Tbs. fresh lemon juice
- 2 Tbs. sorghum syrup
- ½ Tbs. finely chopped fresh flat-leaf parsley
  Kosher salt

MAKE THE SOUP

Position a rack in the center of the oven and heat the oven to 350°F. Place the sweet potatoes on a baking sheet, and bake until tender, 40 to 50 minutes. When cool enough to handle, peel and cut the sweet potatoes into ¾-inch pieces. Set aside.

In a large (4-quart) saucepan, heat the butter and oil over medium low heat. Add the onion and cook, stirring occasionally, until softened, 10 to 15 minutes.

Add the reserved potatoes, chicken broth, and 1 tsp. salt. Bring to a boil over medium-high heat, and then reduce the heat to medium-low or low and simmer for 15 minutes. Let cool briefly.

Working in batches, purée the soup in a blender until smooth. Strain through a fine-mesh sieve into a clean saucepan. Add the heavy cream and buttermilk, and season to taste with salt.

MAKE THE DUCK CRACKLINGS

Slice the duck skin into ½-inch strips and place in a 10-inch heavy-duty straight-sided sauté pan. Add ¼ cup water, the bay leaf, and 1 tsp. salt. Bring to a boil over medium high heat, reduce the heat to maintain a simmer, and cook until the water evaporates and the skin is golden-brown, 10 to 15 minutes. With a slotted spoon, transfer the skin to paper towels to drain. Season to taste with salt and let cool. Chop coarsely.

MAKE THE SORGHUM BUTTER

In a 1-quart heavy-duty saucepan, heat the butter over medium heat until the milk solids turn golden-brown, 5 to 6 minutes. Remove from the heat, and immediately add the lemon juice, sorghum, parsley, and ¼ tsp. salt.

To serve, reheat the soup, if necessary. Ladle the soup into 6 bowls. Spoon about 1 Tbs. sorghum brown butter over the top and sprinkle about 2 Tbs. of duck cracklings over each.

roasted butternut squash salad with pears and stilton

Using just the top half of the squash creates rounds of the same size for even roasting and a pretty salad. **Serves 4**

1   **large butternut squash (about 3 lb.)**

5   **Tbs. extra-virgin olive oil**

½   **tsp. chopped fresh rosemary**

    Kosher salt and freshly ground black pepper

6   **slices thick-cut bacon, cut into ½-inch pieces**

1½   **Tbs. balsamic vinegar**

1   **tsp. Dijon mustard**

1   **medium head escarole (about 1 lb.), trimmed and torn into 1½-inch pieces (about 10 lightly packed cups)**

2   **medium firm-ripe pears (Bartlett or Anjou), peeled, cored, and sliced ⅛ inch thick**

6   **oz. Stilton, cut into 8 wedges**

Position a rack in the center of the oven and heat the oven to 450°F.

Cut off the narrow top portion of the squash close to where it widens (reserve the base for another use). Peel and slice it into 12 thin (about ¼-inch) rounds.

Brush both sides of the squash with 1 Tbs. of the oil and spread in a single layer on a large rimmed baking sheet. Sprinkle with the rosemary, ½ tsp. salt, and ½ tsp. pepper. Roast, turning once, until softened and browned, about 25 minutes.

Meanwhile, in a 12-inch skillet, cook the bacon over medium heat, stirring occasionally, until crisp, 5 to 7 minutes. Transfer with a slotted spoon to paper towels to drain.

In a small bowl, whisk together the vinegar, mustard, ½ tsp. salt, and ½ tsp. pepper. Slowly whisk in the remaining 4 Tbs. oil and season with more salt and pepper to taste.

In a large bowl, toss the escarole and pears with enough of the vinaigrette to coat lightly. Season to taste with salt and pepper.

Arrange the squash on 4 large dinner plates. Top each with a mound of the escarole and pears and sprinkle with the bacon. Tuck 2 wedges of Stilton into each salad and serve.

roasted beet salad with crumbled feta & spicy pepitas

Pure color was the inspiration for this salad: crimson beets paired with a slaw of brilliant red cabbage and red onions, with a crumble of snow-white feta on top. **Serves 8**

FOR THE BEETS

- **1** bunch small beets (4 to 5), trimmed and scrubbed
- **2** to 3 sprigs fresh thyme or rosemary, or 3 fresh bay leaves
- **½** tsp. kosher or sea salt
- **1** Tbs. olive oil

FOR THE VINAIGRETTE

- **1** Tbs. Dijon mustard
- **2** Tbs. sherry vinegar
- **2** Tbs. fresh lemon juice
  Kosher salt and freshly ground black pepper
- **¼** cup extra-virgin olive oil

FOR THE SPICY PEPITAS

- **6** oz. pepitas (hulled pumpkin seeds; see Test Kitchen, p. 141, or find them in natural-foods stores)
- **1** tsp. corn or peanut oil
- **1** tsp. pure chile powder (such as New Mexico or ancho)
- **¾** tsp. kosher salt

FOR THE SALAD

- **4** cups very thinly sliced red cabbage (from 1 very small head)
- **1** medium red onion, very thinly sliced
- **4** oz. (4 cups) mixed baby greens
- **6** oz. feta cheese, crumbled (about ½ cup)
- **6** oz. spicy pepitas (1 generous cup)

Roast the beets: Position a rack in the center of the oven and heat the oven to 400°F. Line a rimmed baking sheet with foil. Put the beets, herbs, salt, and a drizzle of olive oil in the center; toss the beets to coat. Fold the foil into a loose-fitting but tightly sealed packet around the beets. Roast the packet on the baking sheet until the beets are tender, about 1 hour and 20 minutes. Let the beets cool completely in the foil. When cool, use a paring knife to peel and slice the beets into wedges (6 to 8 per beet). The beets can be roasted up to 2 days ahead and refrigerated.

Make the vinaigrette: In a small bowl, combine the mustard, vinegar, lemon juice, ¼ teaspoon salt, and a few grinds of pepper. Slowly whisk in the oil.

Toast the pepitas: Heat oven to 375°F. In a small bowl, toss pepitas with corn oil, chile powder, and kosher salt. Spread evenly on a rimmed baking sheet and roast at 375°F until golden and fragrant, 6 to 8 minutes (you'll hear them popping). Let cool completely on the baking sheet. If making ahead, store in an airtight container.

Make the salad: Combine the cabbage and onion in a medium bowl and set aside. Up to an hour before serving, add the beet wedges to the cabbage and onions; toss gently with half of the vinaigrette.

Just before serving, add the baby greens, half of the feta, and half of the pepitas; toss with the remaining feta and pepitas.

roasted chicken, chickpea, and cauliflower salad

This party-worthy main-course salad is a wonderful combination of roasted chicken thighs and cauliflower, chickpeas, pickled red onions, olives, and peppery arugula. It's simultaneously refreshing and filling.
Serves 6

- 8 boneless, skinless chicken thighs (about 1½ lb.)
- 1 medium head cauliflower, cut into 2-inch florets
- 5 Tbs. extra-virgin olive oil
   Kosher salt and freshly ground black pepper
- ½ small red onion, halved lengthwise and thinly sliced crosswise
- 3 Tbs. Champagne vinegar
- 1 tsp. Dijon mustard
- 2 cups Chickpeas with Bay Leaves and Herbs (recipe at right) or rinsed, drained, canned chickpeas
- ¼ cup green olives (preferably picho-line), pitted and quartered
- ¼ cup lightly packed fresh flat-leaf parsley leaves
- 5 oz. (5 cups) baby arugula

Position racks in the upper and lower thirds of the oven and heat the oven to 425°F.
Spread the chicken and cauliflower in single layers on separate large rimmed baking sheets. Toss each with 1 Tbs. of the oil, 1 tsp. salt, and several grinds of pepper. Roast with the chicken in the top third of the oven, switching positions and rotating the pans halfway through, until the cauliflower is golden and crisp-tender, about 20 minutes, and the chicken reaches 165°F, 20 to 25 minutes. Tent the chicken with foil to keep warm.
Meanwhile, combine the onion with the vinegar and ¼ tsp. salt in a small bowl. Let sit until the onion has mellowed and turned a vibrant pink, 10 to 12 minutes.
Drain the onion over a small bowl. Whisk the mustard, ¼ tsp. salt, and a few grinds of pepper into the vinegar. Slowly whisk in the remaining 3 Tbs. oil.
Slice the chicken crosswise ½ inch thick. In a large bowl, combine the chicken, cauliflower, onion, chickpeas, olives, and parsley. Toss with the dressing, and then season to taste with salt and pepper. Add the arugula and gently toss again before serving.

chickpeas with bay leaves and herbs

Yields about 6 cups chickpeas and 2½ cups cooking liquid

- 1 lb. dried chickpeas (about 2½ cups)
- 1 small yellow onion, peeled and quartered
- 3 large sprigs fresh flat-leaf parsley
- 3 large sprigs fresh thyme
- 2 bay leaves
   Kosher salt

Put the chickpeas in a large bowl, cover with cold water by a couple of inches, and refrigerate for at least 6 and up to 24 hours.
Drain and rinse the chickpeas. Transfer to a 6-quart pot. Tie the onion, herb sprigs, and bay leaves in a piece of cheesecloth and add the bundle to the pot. Add 10 cups cold water and bring to a boil, skimming off any foam. Turn the heat down to maintain a gentle simmer and cook until just tender, about 1 hour.
Add 2 tsp. salt and continue cooking until the chickpeas are fully tender and creamy on the inside but retain their shape, 15 to 30 minutes more.
Drain the chickpeas, reserving the cooking liquid; discard the herb bundle. Let the chickpeas and the reserved liquid cool to room temperature. Refrigerate in separate airtight containers for up to 5 days.

roasted potato salad with bell peppers, roasted corn & tomatoes

Roasted potatoes have a crunchy-on-the-outside, soft-on-the-inside texture that makes them perfect in salads. Try this one with grilled pork chops or roasted pork tenderloin. **Serves 6**

2 lb. small red-skinned potatoes or small Yukon Gold potatoes, washed and cut into ¾-inch chunks

½ cup plus 1 tsp. extra-virgin olive oil

Kosher salt and freshly ground black pepper

1 ear fresh corn, in the husk

2 cups red, yellow, or orange cherry tomatoes (or a combination), halved

½ red bell pepper, cut into ¼-inch dice

½ green bell pepper, cut into ¼-inch dice

½ small red onion, cut into ¼-inch dice

½ yellow bell pepper, cut into ¼-inch dice

½ cup chopped fresh basil

2 small cloves garlic, finely chopped

3 Tbs. red-wine vinegar

Position a rack in the center of the oven and heat the oven to 450°F. Spread the potatoes on a heavy-duty rimmed baking sheet. Drizzle with 3 Tbs. olive oil, sprinkle with 1 tsp. kosher salt, and several grinds of pepper, and roll the potatoes around to evenly coat them with the oil. Spread the potatoes in a single layer, preferably with a cut side down. Roast them until they're tender when pierced with a fork, 20 to 30 minutes, depending on the potatoes. The potatoes should be browned on the sides touching the pan.

Loosen the potatoes from the pan with a thin spatula and transfer them to a large serving bowl.

While the potatoes are roasting, prepare and roast the corn. Remove the husk and put the corn on a small baking sheet. Drizzle 1 tsp. of the oil onto the corn and rub it over all the kernels. Sprinkle with kosher salt and pepper. Roast, turning the cob occasionally, until the corn kernels are light brown in a few spots, about 20 minutes. Let the corn cool. Cut the kernels from the cob.

Add the corn, tomatoes, peppers, onion, basil, and garlic to the potatoes. Toss gently.

Whisk the remaining ¼ cup oil and the vinegar together and add to the salad. Toss again. Season with kosher salt and pepper to taste and serve immediately.

roasted broccoli and farro salad with feta

Roasting the broccoli gives it a cara-melized edge that pairs beautifully with the earthy grains and creamy feta in this salad. Feel free to substitute cauli-flower for the broccoli. **Yields 5 cups; serves 4**

Kosher salt

¾ cup farro (whole grain or pearled; see Test Kitchen, p. 132, for more information)

1 lb. broccoli

3 Tbs. extra-virgin olive oil

½ cup crumbled feta

2 scallions, thinly sliced

Pinch crushed red pepper flakes

2 Tbs. coarsely chopped fresh flat-leaf parsley

1 Tbs. red-wine vinegar; more as needed

Position a rack in the center of the oven and heat the oven to 400°F. In a 4-quart saucepan, bring 2 quarts of well-salted water to a boil over high heat. Boil the farro in the water until tender, 20 to 30 minutes for pearled and 45 to 60 minutes for whole grain. Drain well and transfer to a large bowl.

Meanwhile, remove the broccoli crown from the stem and cut into bite-size florets. Peel and halve the stem length-wise, then cut crosswise into ¼-inch-thick slices. On a rimmed baking sheet, toss the broccoli florets and stems with 2 Tbs. of the olive oil. Roast until tender and browned in spots, about 20 minutes.

Add the broccoli, feta, scallions, red pepper flakes, and parsley to the farro. Sprinkle with the vinegar and 1 tsp. salt and toss. Drizzle with the remaining 1 Tbs. olive oil and toss. Season to taste with more vinegar and salt. Serve warm or at room temperature.

Pan-Roasted Sunchokes and Artichoke Hearts
Pan-Roasted Sunchokes and Artichoke
Hearts with Lemon–Herb Butter, p. 20

Vegetables

Roasted veggies get a boost with flavored butters, creamy sauces, and more.

the recipes

sweet potato oven fries with fry sauce

Delicious on their own, these smoky, slightly sweet fries are downright dangerous when dipped into a zesty spin on fry sauce, a ketchup-and-mayonnaise-based condiment popular in Utah, Idaho, and the Pacific Northwest. **Serves 4 to 6**

	Cooking spray
1	lb. sweet potatoes (about 1 large)
2	large egg whites
1	tsp. smoked paprika
½	tsp. ground cumin
	Kosher salt
¼	cup mayonnaise
2	Tbs. ketchup
1	tsp. lemon juice
½	tsp. soy sauce
½	tsp. Worcestershire sauce
2	drops hot sauce, such as Sriracha

Position racks in the bottom and top thirds of the oven and heat the oven to 425°F. Spray two baking sheets with cooking spray.

Peel and cut the potatoes into approximately 2-inch lengths, and then cut each piece lengthwise into ¼-inch-wide slices. Lay the slices flat and cut them into ¼-inch strips, so you have ¼ x ¼ x 2-inch sticks.

Whisk the egg whites with the smoked paprika, cumin, and 1 tsp. salt in a medium bowl. Toss the potatoes in the mixture to thoroughly coat. Spread them on the baking sheets in a single layer so that they're not touching.

Roast the sweet potatoes until sizzling and starting to brown on the bottom, about 10 minutes. With a spatula, carefully loosen the fries and shake the baking sheet to flip them. Rotate the placement of the baking sheets in the oven and continue to bake until the fries are lightly browned, sizzling vigorously, and tender all the way through, another 8 to 9 minutes. Sprinkle to taste with more salt.

Meanwhile, make the fry sauce. In a small bowl, stir the mayonnaise, ketchup, lemon juice, soy sauce, Worcestershire sauce, and hot sauce. Adjust the seasonings until the sauce tastes zesty but balanced.

Serve the oven fries immediately with the fry sauce.

Tossing sweet potatoes with egg whites before roasting ensures that they come out with a nicely browned coating.

pan-roasted brussels sprout gratin with shallots and rosemary

This rich, creamy side dish is a guaranteed crowd-pleaser. Brussels sprouts, pan-roasted in brown butter until tender and nutty, are mixed with sweet, earthy Gruyère and topped with crisp breadcrumbs. For a casual dinner, serve it straight from the skillet. **Serves 6 to 8**

1½ lb. Brussels sprouts, trimmed

2 large shallots, halved

4 Tbs. unsalted butter

Kosher salt and freshly ground black pepper

1¼ cups heavy cream

3¼ oz. (1¼ cups) finely grated Gruyère

¼ tsp. freshly grated nutmeg

⅛ tsp. cayenne

¾ cup panko

½ cup finely grated Parmigiano-Reggiano

2 tsp. finely chopped fresh rosemary

Position a rack in the center of the oven and heat the oven to 375°F. In a food processor fitted with the slicing blade, slice the Brussels sprouts and shallots.

In a 12-inch oven-safe skillet, melt the butter over medium heat. Continue to cook the butter until it begins to brown and smell nutty. Set aside 1 Tbs. of the browned butter in a medium bowl.

Add the Brussels sprouts, shallots, 2 tsp. salt, and ½ tsp. pepper to the pan and toss to combine. Cook, stirring occasionally, until the Brussels sprouts and shallots begin to soften and brown in spots, about 6 minutes. Remove the pan from the heat.

Meanwhile, in a 2-quart saucepan over medium heat, combine the cream, Gruyère, nutmeg, cayenne, and ¼ tsp. salt. Heat until the cheese is melted, whisking occasionally, about 4 minutes. Do not boil. Add the sauce to the Brussels sprouts, carefully stirring to combine.

Add the panko, Parmigiano, rosemary, and a pinch of salt to the reserved butter and mix thoroughly. Top the sprout mixture with the panko mixture.

Bake until the crumbs are browned and the Brussels sprouts are tender, 10 to 15 minutes. Let cool for about 5 minutes before serving.

For an elegant presentation, transfer the sprout mixture to a ceramic baking dish before adding the panko and baking.

roasted sweet potatoes with apples and maple-sage butter

Roasted sweet potatoes have a lush, tender texture and concentrated flavor. When paired with maple syrup and apples, they make a deliciously sweet side that works with anything from pan-seared steak to roasted turkey. **Serves 6 to 8**

1½ to 2 lb. sweet potatoes, peeled, halved crosswise, and cut into ¾-inch-thick wedges

2 Tbs. olive oil

Kosher salt and freshly ground black pepper

2 Tbs. unsalted butter

1 medium-large tart green or red apple, quartered, cored, cut into 16 wedges, wedges halved crosswise

1 Tbs. chopped fresh sage

1½ tsp. fresh lemon juice

1 tsp. pure maple syrup

Position a rack in the top third of the oven and heat the oven to 475°F.

In a large bowl, toss the sweet potatoes with the oil, 1 tsp. salt, and a few grinds of black pepper. Spread the potatoes in a single layer on a large rimmed baking sheet. Roast for 10 minutes; then flip the potatoes and continue roasting until tender and browned in spots, about 5 minutes more.

While the potatoes roast, heat the butter in a 12-inch skillet over medium-high heat until melted and beginning to brown, 1 to 2 minutes. Add the apples in a single layer and brown on both sides, 1 to 2 minutes per side. Add the sage and stir until wilted, about 30 seconds. Off the heat, stir in the lemon juice and maple syrup. With a spatula, scrape the apples and butter into the bowl used for tossing the potatoes.

When the potatoes are done, add them to the apples and gently combine with the spatula.

Season to taste with salt and pepper, and serve.

roasted garlic

You can double or triple this recipe easily. It's great served simply on toasted bread. For other ways to use it, see below. **Yields 1 cup mashed roasted garlic**

10	medium heads garlic
¼	cup extra-virgin olive oil
	Kosher salt and freshly ground black pepper
4	sprigs fresh thyme

Position a rack in the center of the oven and heat the oven to 400°F.

Slice ½ inch from the top of each head of garlic. Arrange the garlic cut side up on a large sheet of heavy-duty aluminum foil. Drizzle with 3 Tbs. of the oil and season with ¼ tsp. each salt and pepper. Add the thyme sprigs and wrap the foil tightly to make a packet.

Roast until the cloves are light golden-brown and very soft, about 1½ hours. Remove from the oven and let cool.

To remove the garlic from the heads, squeeze the cloves from the bottom into a small bowl. Using a fork, mash the garlic with the remaining tablespoon of oil.

You can store the roasted garlic in an airtight container in the refrigerator for up to 2 weeks, or freeze for up to 1 month.

five ways with roasted garlic

Roasting garlic mellows and sweetens its flavor and adds a delicious caramelized note. Here are five simple ideas for using roasted garlic.

Garlic-Roasted Chicken Smear roasted garlic under the skin of a chicken, season with salt and pepper, and roast until it's golden-brown and cooked through.

Garlicky Vegetable Soup Deepen the flavor of your favorite vegetable soup recipe by stirring in some mashed roasted garlic.

Roasted-Garlic Risotto Make a basic risotto using olive oil, butter, arborio rice, white wine, broth, and Parmigiano-Reggiano. Stir in roasted garlic and more butter in the last 5 minutes of cooking.

White Bean and Garlic Bruschetta Mash cooked white beans with some roasted garlic, a little chopped fresh rosemary, and finely grated pecorino. Spoon onto toasted slices of bread, drizzle with extra-virgin olive oil, and serve as a snack or appetizer.

Spicy Garlic Shrimp Sauté peeled, deveined shrimp with extra-virgin olive oil, sliced onion, roasted garlic, crushed red pepper flakes, and smoked paprika. Add a splash of Spanish sherry and serve over steamed white rice.

pan-roasted sunchokes and artichoke hearts with lemon-herb butter

If you don't have dry vermouth, use dry white wine instead.

Serves 4 to 6

- 2 Tbs. extra-virgin olive oil
- 1 lb. medium sunchokes, scrubbed and cut lengthwise into ¾-inch-thick wedges

  Kosher salt
- 8 oz. frozen quartered artichoke hearts, thawed
- 2 Tbs. finely chopped shallot
- 3 Tbs. dry vermouth
- 1 Tbs. fresh lemon juice
- 2 Tbs. cold unsalted butter, cut into small pieces
- 1 Tbs. chopped fresh flat-leaf parsley
- 2 tsp. chopped fresh tarragon

  Freshly ground black pepper

Position a rack in the upper third of the oven and heat the oven to 400°F.

In a 12-inch ovenproof skillet, heat the oil over medium-high heat until shimmering hot. Add the sunchokes and ¼ tsp. salt; cook, flipping as needed, until well browned on both cut sides, 2 to 3 minutes per side. Add the artichoke hearts and ¼ tsp. salt; cook, stirring occasionally, until lightly browned, 2 to 3 minutes.

Move the skillet to the oven and roast until the sunchokes are tender, about 20 minutes. Transfer the vegetables to a bowl and cover to keep warm.

Set the skillet over medium heat, add the shallot and cook, stirring with a wooden spoon, until softened and lightly browned, 1 to 2 minutes. Add the vermouth and cook, stirring and scraping the bottom of the pan to loosen any brown bits, until the vermouth has almost evaporated.

Reduce the heat to low, add the lemon juice, and then the butter one piece at a time, swirling the pan to melt the butter before adding the next piece. Stir in the parsley and tarragon. Return the vegetables to the pan and toss to reheat and coat in the butter. Season to taste with salt and pepper before serving.

roasted fennel with asiago and thyme

Roasting fennel brings out its mellow sweetness; a sprinkling of thyme and grated Asiago dresses it up. If you double this recipe, use two baking sheets so the fennel isn't too crowded to brown. **Serves 4**

2   **large fennel bulbs (about 2 lb. total)**

2   **Tbs. extra-virgin olive oil**
    Kosher salt and freshly ground black pepper

1   **tsp. minced fresh thyme**

⅓   **cup packed grated Asiago**

Position a rack in the top third of the oven, put a large heavy-duty rimmed baking sheet on the rack, and heat the oven to 500°F.

Trim the fennel, quarter each bulb vertically, and trim away most of the core, leaving just enough to hold the layers intact. Slice each quarter into 4 wedges.

In a medium bowl, toss the fennel with the olive oil, ½ tsp. salt, and ½ tsp. pepper. Remove the baking sheet from the oven and quickly spread the fennel on the sheet, with the largest pieces toward the edges of the pan. Roast until the fennel pieces are almost tender and the bottoms are lightly browned, about 18 minutes.

Flip the fennel, sprinkle with the thyme and then the Asiago, and continue roasting until the cheese is melted and golden, 3 to 5 minutes more. With a spatula, transfer the fennel and any lacy, golden cheese bits to a serving dish.

roasted turnips with maple and cardamom

An intriguing sauce laced with coriander and cardamom gives the dish surprising complexity. It's great served alongside roast turkey or pork. **Serves 8**

3½ lb. purple-top turnips, peeled and cut into ¾-inch dice (10 cups)

3 Tbs. vegetable oil
   Kosher salt

2 Tbs. unsalted butter

3 Tbs. pure maple syrup

¼ tsp. pure vanilla extract
   Generous pinch crushed red pepper flakes

¼ tsp. ground coriander

⅛ tsp. ground cardamom

1 tsp. fresh lemon juice

1 Tbs. finely chopped fresh cilantro (or a mix of parsley and mint)

Position racks in the top and bottom thirds of the oven and heat the oven to 475°F. Line two large, heavy-duty rimmed baking sheets with foil. In a mixing bowl, combine the turnips, oil, and 1½ tsp. salt. Toss to coat well. Divide the turnips between the two pans and spread evenly in one layer. Roast for 20 minutes. With a large spatula, flip the turnips. Swap the pans' positions and roast until tender and nicely browned on a few sides, 15 to 20 minutes. (The turnips on the lower rack may be done sooner than those on the upper rack.)

Meanwhile, melt the butter in a small sauce-pan over low heat. Whisk in the maple syrup, vanilla, and red pepper flakes, and then the coriander and cardamom, until the sauce is heated, 30 seconds. Remove the pan from the heat.

Place the turnips in a large mixing bowl. Gently reheat the sauce, if necessary, and stir in the lemon juice. With a heatproof spatula, toss the sauce with the turnips. Add half of the cilantro and salt to taste and toss again. Transfer to a warm serving dish and garnish with the remaining cilantro.

Make Ahead

This dish can be made a day ahead. To reheat, put the dressed turnips (without the cilantro) in a large nonstick skillet. Cover and heat gently over medium-low heat until warm, stirring occasionally, about 15 minutes. Add the cilantro and season to taste just before serving.

pan-roasted carrots with leeks, pancetta, and thyme

The carrots and leeks in this rich, savory side dish get a double dose of browning—first from searing, then from roasting. Try to find thin leeks with long white and light-green parts to match the shape and size of the carrots. Serve with a roasted leg of lamb for a special occasion or with a simple roasted pork loin for a Sunday meal. **Serves 4**

3	to 4 very thin slices pancetta (about 1 oz.)
2½	Tbs. unsalted butter
1½	tsp. olive oil
1	lb. leeks (about 3 medium), white and light-green parts only, trimmed and quartered lengthwise
1	lb. medium carrots, quartered
	Kosher salt
⅓	cup plus 2 Tbs. dry white wine, such as Sauvignon Blanc
1¼	cups lower-salt chicken broth
1	tsp. chopped fresh thyme
½	tsp. ground coriander

Position a rack in the center of the oven and heat the oven to 425°F. In a 12-inch oven-safe skillet, cook the pancetta over medium-low heat until brown, turning as necessary, 5 to 8 minutes. Transfer the pancetta to a plate lined with paper towels (it will crisp as it cools); remove the skillet from the heat and cool slightly.

Put the skillet over medium heat and add 1½ Tbs. of the butter and the olive oil. When the butter has melted, arrange the leek and carrot pieces on the bottom of the pan in a snug single layer. Season with ½ tsp. salt and cook, undisturbed, until the bottoms of the vegetables are browned (the leeks may be slightly darker than the carrots), about 5 minutes.

Using tongs, flip the vegetables and add ⅓ cup of the wine. Continue to cook undisturbed until the wine has almost evaporated, 2 to 3 minutes.

Add the chicken broth, half of the thyme, and the coriander, and transfer the skillet to the oven.

Roast until the carrots are tender when pierced with a fork, about 30 minutes.

Transfer the vegetables to a warm platter. Put the skillet over medium-high heat (use caution; the handle is hot), add the remaining 2 Tbs. wine, and stir for a few seconds, scraping up any browned bits. Remove the skillet from the heat, add the remaining 1 Tbs. butter and ½ tsp. thyme, and stir to melt the butter. Pour the sauce over the vegetables, crumble the pancetta over top, and serve.

roasted brussels sprouts with wild mushrooms and cream

If you're used to simple steamed or boiled sprouts, this rich, luxurious dish will be a delicious surprise.
Serves 6

- 1½ lb. Brussels sprouts, trimmed and halved lengthwise (5 cups)
- 5 Tbs. olive oil
  Kosher salt
- 3 Tbs. unsalted butter
- ¾ lb. wild mushrooms, such as chanterelles or hedgehogs, halved if small or cut into 1-inch wedges (about 4½ cups)
- 1 large shallot, thinly sliced (½ cup)
- ¼ cup dry white wine
- 1 cup heavy cream
  Freshly ground black pepper

Position a rack in the center of the oven and heat the oven to 450°F.

Put the Brussels sprouts on a rimmed baking sheet, and drizzle with 3 Tbs. of the olive oil; toss to coat. Spread the sprouts in an even layer and season generously with salt. Roast until tender and browned, about 25 minutes. Remove from the oven and set aside.

Heat a 12-inch skillet over high heat. When the pan is hot, add 1 Tbs. of the olive oil and 2 Tbs. of the butter. When the butter has melted, add the mushrooms in an even layer, and cook, stirring occasionally, until the mushrooms are golden-brown and tender and the mushroom liquid (if any) has evaporated, 5 to 8 minutes.

Season to taste with salt and transfer to a plate. (The recipe may be prepared to this point up to 8 hours ahead.)

Set the skillet over medium-high heat and add the remaining 1 Tbs. olive oil and 1 Tbs. butter. When the butter has melted, add the shallot, season with a pinch of salt, and cook, stirring occasionally, until tender and golden, 3 to 4 minutes. Add the wine and cook until reduced by half, about 1 minute.

Return the mushrooms to the pan and add the Brussels sprouts and cream. Stir in a few grinds of pepper and continue to cook, stirring occasionally, until the cream thickens and coats the vegetables nicely, 3 to 4 minutes. Season to taste with salt and pepper. Serve immediately.

basic roasted green beans

You can jazz up this basic recipe by adding herbs and flavored oil when you toss the green beans with salt and pepper before roasting. **Serves 4**

- 1 lb. green beans, stem ends trimmed
- 1 to 3 Tbs. extra-virgin olive oil
- ½ tsp. kosher salt; more to taste
  Freshly ground black pepper
  Fresh lemon juice (optional)

Position a rack in the center of the oven and heat the oven to 475°F. Line a heavy-duty rimmed baking sheet with parchment. In a medium bowl, toss the green beans with enough of the olive oil to coat generously, the salt, and a few grinds of pepper.

Turn the beans out onto the baking sheet and arrange them so that they are evenly spaced. If the beans cover the baking sheet sparsely, arrange them toward the edges of the baking sheet for the best browning. Roast the beans until they're tender, a bit shriveled, and slightly browned, about 15 minutes.

Return the green beans to the bowl in which you tossed them with the oil, or put them in a clean serving bowl. If they seem a bit dry, drizzle them with a little oil. Season to taste with salt, pepper, and lemon juice or another flavoring, if using.

honey-roasted radishes

Roasting mellows radishes' sharp bite, as does a touch of honey and delicate white balsamic vinegar. Wilted radish tops add great texture and a pop of color to the dish. Serve with lamb, steak, or pan-roasted trout. **Serves 4**

- **1¾** **lb. radishes (about 2 bunches)**
- **2** **Tbs. honey**
- **1** **Tbs. unsalted butter, melted**
- **1** **Tbs. white balsamic vinegar**
-    **Kosher salt and freshly ground black pepper**

Position a rack in the center of the oven, set a 12-inch oven-proof skillet (preferably cast iron) on the rack, and heat the oven to 450°F.

Remove and reserve the tops from the radishes. Trim the radishes and then halve or quarter them lengthwise, depending on their size. Trim and discard the stems from the tops, wash the leaves thoroughly, and pat dry or dry in a salad spinner.

In a medium bowl, combine the honey, melted butter, balsamic vinegar, ½ tsp. kosher salt, and ½ tsp. freshly ground black pepper. Add the radishes and toss until coated. Transfer to the hot skillet, spread in a single layer, and roast, stirring occasionally, until the radishes are crisp-tender, 15 to 20 minutes. Remove from the oven, add the radish leaves, and toss until the leaves are just wilted; serve.

roasted squash with pimentón and manchego

This side dish gets a dose of Spanish flavor from smoky pimentón (Spanish paprika) and aged Manchego. **Serves 4**

1½ lb. assorted summer squash, washed

    Kosher salt

  1 cup medium-diced yellow onion

  1 Tbs. extra-virgin olive oil

1½ tsp. hot pimentón

  1 cup coarsely grated Manchego

Position a rack in the center of the oven and heat the oven to 450°F. Trim the squash and cut into 1-inch chunks. In a colander, toss the squash with 1 tsp. kosher salt and drain for 30 minutes; transfer to a large bowl.

Toss the squash with the onion, olive oil, and pimentón. Arrange in single layer on a rimmed baking sheet. Roast until the squash is lightly golden, about 20 minutes, then flip and continue to roast until the squash and onion are golden-brown and tender, about 20 minutes more.

Sprinkle with the Manchego, toss gently, and serve.

a cross between a lemon and an orange

Meyer lemons are sweeter than standard lemons and have slightly floral undertones.

When shopping for Meyers, look for smooth, tight skin and an orange hue. The lemons should be firm but give under slight pressure and should feel a little bit heavy for their size. They will smell sweet and floral, like orange blossoms.

Meyer lemons will keep for a few days at room temperature and up to a month in the refrigerator. Their juice can be frozen for up to 6 months.

roasted root vegetables with meyer lemon

This versatile side dish is delicious with just about any kind of meat, poultry, or fish. For the vegetables to roast evenly, the turnips, which cook more quickly than the carrots and parsnips, are cut slightly larger. **Serves 4 to 6**

1 **lb. carrots (about 5 medium),** peeled, trimmed, cut crosswise into 3-inch lengths, then cut lengthwise into ½-inch-thick pieces

1 **lb. parsnips (about 5 large),** peeled, trimmed, cut crosswise into 3-inch lengths, then cut lengthwise into ½-inch-thick pieces, cores removed

1 **lb. medium purple-top turnips (2 or 3),** scrubbed, trimmed, and cut into ¾-inch wedges

1 **Meyer lemon,** top and bottom ends trimmed, quartered lengthwise and sliced crosswise ⅛ inch thick, seeds removed

¼ **cup extra-virgin olive oil**

1 **Tbs. finely chopped fresh rosemary**

2 **tsp. minced fresh garlic**

½ **tsp. ground cumin**
   Kosher salt and freshly ground black pepper

Position a rack in the center of the oven and heat the oven to 450°F. Line a large rimmed baking sheet with heavy-duty aluminum foil.

In a large bowl, combine the carrots, parsnips, turnips, lemon, oil, rosemary, garlic, cumin, 1 tsp. salt, and ½ tsp. pepper; toss to coat. Spread in an even layer on the baking sheet and roast, tossing once, until tender when pierced with a fork and golden-brown on the edges, 40 to 50 minutes.

Season to taste with salt and pepper and serve.

spicy asian roasted broccoli and snap peas

Bright accents like cilantro, miso, chiles, and orange zest punctuate the deep, sweet flavor of roasted vegetables. If you have trouble finding fresh Thai chiles (also called bird chiles), try using the same amount of the dried version. **Serves 4**

5 cups broccoli florets (from about 2 broccoli crowns)

3 cups (about 12 oz.) fresh sugar snap peas

6 to 8 red or orange fresh Thai chiles, stems trimmed

3 Tbs. extra-virgin olive oil

2 Tbs. plus 1 tsp. toasted sesame oil

1 tsp. kosher salt

2 Tbs. fresh cilantro leaves, chopped

1½ Tbs. light-colored (white or yellow) miso

1 Tbs. honey

2 tsp. sambal oelek (Asian chile paste)

1 tsp. finely grated orange zest

1 tsp. grated fresh ginger

1 clove garlic, minced

Position a rack in the center of the oven and heat the oven to 450°F.

Put the broccoli, peas, and chiles in a large bowl; toss with 2 Tbs. of the olive oil and 2 Tbs. of the sesame oil. Sprinkle with salt and toss again. Transfer the vegetables to a 10x15-inch Pyrex® dish and roast, stirring once, until the peas are lightly browned and the broccoli tops are quite dark in spots, about 22 minutes.

Meanwhile, in a small bowl, whisk the remaining 1 Tbs. olive oil, 1 tsp. sesame oil, cilantro, miso, honey, sambal oelek, orange zest, ginger, and garlic. Pour the mixture over the roasted vegetables and toss to coat. Remove the chiles (or leave them in for color but warn diners not to eat them). Serve immediately.

> **Fiery Thai chiles don't mellow when cooked. Their main purpose in this dish is to add a colorful contrast—and some heat.**

Sear-Roasted Halibut with
Blood Orange Salsa, p. 34

Fish & Shellfish

These quick and delicious roasted seafood dishes are perfect for any night of the week.

the recipes

garlicky shrimp with basil

This recipe gets a double punch of garlic from infused garlic oil and gently cooked garlic slices. Make sure to serve it with lots of crusty bread for polishing off the flavorful juices. You can roast the shrimp in one large baking dish or in individual servings. **Serves 4 to 6**

⅔ cup extra-virgin olive oil

6 to 8 large cloves garlic (1½ oz.), halved lengthwise, peeled, germs removed, and sliced ⅛ inch thick

1½ lb. shrimp (20 to 25 per lb., about 32), peeled, deveined, and patted dry

⅓ cup dry white wine

Kosher salt and freshly ground black pepper

¼ cup thinly sliced fresh basil

1 tsp. finely grated lemon zest

Position a rack in the center of the oven and heat the oven to 425°F.

Put the oil and garlic in a small (8-inch) skillet and set over medium-low heat. Cook, stirring occasionally, until the garlic just begins to turn golden, 8 to 12 minutes. Strain the garlic and oil through a sieve set over a bowl; spread the garlic slices on a paper-towel-lined plate to drain.

Put the shrimp in a gratin or baking dish that is about 7x9 inches. Pour the garlic oil and wine over the shrimp and season with 1 tsp. salt and ¼ tsp. pepper.

Roast, stirring once, until the shrimp are pink, opaque, and cooked through, 8 to 12 minutes. Sprinkle the garlic slices, basil, and lemon zest over the shrimp, stir to combine, and serve immediately.

miso-roasted atlantic mackerel

Mackerel's rich, strong flavor pairs well with complex ingredients like miso and soy and is complemented by citrus and bright vinaigrettes. **Serves 4**

- ¼ **cup white or yellow miso**
- ¼ **cup honey**
- 1 **Tbs. toasted Asian sesame oil**
- 2 **tsp. reduced-sodium soy sauce**
- 8 **boneless, skin-on Atlantic mackerel fillets (3½ to 4 oz. each), scaled**
- 2 **to 3 Tbs. vegetable oil; more for the baking sheet**
- 4 **lemon wedges or slices**

In a large bowl, whisk the miso, honey, sesame oil, and soy sauce into a smooth paste. Add the mackerel fillets and toss to coat with the marinade. Marinate for 20 minutes at room temperature. Meanwhile, heat the oven to 350°F.

Wipe the marinade from the skin side of the fillets. Heat 2 Tbs. of the oil in a 12-inch cast-iron or nonstick skillet over medium-high heat. Working in batches to avoid crowding the pan, cook the fillets skin side down until the skin darkens and crisps slightly, 3 to 4 minutes. As each batch finishes, transfer the fillets skin side down to a lightly oiled baking sheet. Add the remaining 1 Tbs. oil to the skillet between batches if it seems dry.

Once all the fillets are seared, put the baking sheet in the oven and bake until the flesh is flaky when poked with a paring knife, 5 minutes. Serve garnished with lemon wedges or slices.

sear-roasted halibut with blood orange salsa

In this dish (shown on p. 30), sear-roasting allows the fish to form a gorgeous crust while keeping the inside moist. **Serves 4**

FOR THE SALSA

- ¾ cup fresh navel or Valencia orange juice (from 2 medium oranges)
- 3 small blood oranges, cut into segments (see Test Kitchen, p. 128), segments cut in half
- 2 Tbs. minced red onion
- 1 Tbs. chopped fresh cilantro
- 1 Tbs. extra-virgin olive oil
- 1 Tbs. finely grated navel or Valencia orange zest (from 2 medium oranges)

  Kosher salt and freshly ground black pepper

FOR THE HALIBUT

- 1 tsp. finely grated navel or Valencia orange zest (from 1 small orange)
- 1 tsp. chopped fresh thyme

  Kosher salt and freshly ground black pepper

- 4 6-oz. skinless halibut fillets
- 3 Tbs. olive oil

Position a rack in the center of the oven and heat the oven to 425°F.

MAKE THE SALSA

In a small saucepan, boil the orange juice over medium heat until reduced to ¼ cup, 8 to 10 minutes. Let cool.

In a medium bowl, combine the reduced orange juice, blood orange segments, onion, cilantro, olive oil, and orange zest. Season to taste with salt and pepper.

COOK THE HALIBUT

In a small bowl, mix the orange zest, thyme, 1½ tsp. salt, and ½ tsp. pepper. Rub the mixture all over the halibut fillets. Heat the oil in a 12-inch ovenproof skillet over medium-high heat. When the oil is shimmering hot, arrange the fillets in the pan. Sear for about 2 minutes without moving; then use a thin slotted metal spatula to lift a piece of fish and check the color. When the fillets are nicely browned, flip them and put the pan in the oven.

Roast until the halibut is just cooked through, 3 to 5 minutes. Remove the pan from the oven and transfer the halibut to serving plates. Spoon some of the salsa over each fillet.

roasted cod with basil pesto and garlic breadcrumbs

Pair the fish with a green salad for a light supper.
Serves 4

- 1 large ripe tomato, cored and very thinly sliced (about ⅛ inch)

  Kosher salt and freshly ground black pepper

- 2 Tbs. extra-virgin olive oil
- 1½ cups coarse fresh white breadcrumbs (from 4 slices of bread, trimmed of crusts)
- 1 small clove garlic, minced
- 1½ lb. cod or haddock, rinsed, patted dry, and cut into 4 even portions
- ⅔ cup Basil Pesto (recipe opposite)

basil pesto

Pesto adds a robust, rich twist to nearly anything from pasta to meat. You can double this recipe and freeze leftovers in an ice cube tray, then pop out the cubes and store in a resealable plastic freezer bag in the freezer for up to 3 months.

Yields about ⅔ cup

- **4 cups lightly packed fresh basil leaves (from about 1 large bunch)**
- **⅓ cup toasted pine nuts**
- **¼ cup lightly packed fresh flat-leaf parsley leaves**
- **1 small clove garlic**
  Kosher salt and freshly ground black pepper
- **¼ extra-virgin olive oil**

Put the basil, pine nuts, parsley, garlic, ½ tsp. salt, and ⅛ tsp. pepper in a food processor. With the machine on, slowly pour the olive oil into the feed tube and process, stopping to scrape the sides of the bowl as needed, until the mixture is very finely chopped and pasty. Season to taste with salt, if you like.

the pesto touch

Six ideas for leftover pesto:

- Toss with zucchini and summer squash seared in a grill pan and top with shavings of Parmigiano-Reggiano.
- Serve dolloped on roasted lamb.
- Spread on sliced ripe fresh tomatoes, top with breadcrumbs, and slide under the broiler to heat.
- Mix a couple of tablespoons of pesto with best-quality extra-virgin olive oil and use as a dip for bread.
- Spread between vegetable layers in a gratin.
- Use as a filling with tomato and ricotta for a vegetable lasagna.

Position a rack in the center of the oven and heat the oven to 450°F. Spread the tomato slices on a large plate and season with ¼ tsp. salt and a few grinds of pepper. Heat a large sauté pan over medium heat for 1 minute. Pour in the olive oil, add the breadcrumbs, and season with ¼ tsp. salt. Cook, stirring, until the breadcrumbs start to turn a light golden-brown, about 4 minutes. Add the garlic and continue to cook, stirring, for another 1 minute. Transfer to a bowl.

Set the fish on a large rimmed baking sheet lined with foil. Season with salt and pepper. Divide the pesto evenly over the fish and top each with two or three tomato slices and the breadcrumbs. Roast until the fish is opaque on the sides and starts to flake, about 10 minutes. Serve immediately.

roasted cod with lemon-parsley crumbs

Simple but satisfying, this comes together quickly thanks to the light, crisp Japanese breadcrumbs called panko, which are available at most supermarkets.

Serves 6

- 1 cup panko breadcrumbs
- 3 Tbs. melted unsalted butter
- 3 Tbs. finely chopped fresh flat-leaf parsley
- 2 tsp. finely grated lemon zest
  Kosher salt and freshly ground black pepper
- 6 1- to 1½-inch-thick cod fillets (about 6 oz. each)

Position a rack in the center of the oven and heat the oven to 425°F.

In a medium bowl, combine the panko, butter, parsley, and lemon zest. Add a pinch of salt and a grind of pepper and stir to evenly distribute the ingredients.

Line a heavy-duty rimmed baking sheet with parchment. Arrange the cod fillets on the baking sheet and season all over with salt and pepper. Divide the panko topping among the fillets, pressing lightly so it adheres. Roast until the breadcrumbs are browned and the fish is mostly opaque (just cooked through), with a trace of translucence in the center (cut into a piece to check), 10 to 12 minutes, depending on the thickness of the fillets. Serve immediately.

> Fold thinner tail pieces of cod under to double their thickness so they don't cook too quickly and dry out.

roasted shrimp with rosemary and thyme

If you like, substitute different herb combinations for the rosemary and thyme — try tarragon and chives or lemon verbena and parsley. Serve the shrimp over rice or with some crusty bread to sop up the fragrant olive oil.

Serves 4

- 6 Tbs. extra-virgin olive oil
- 6 fresh thyme sprigs
- 3 large fresh rosemary sprigs, halved

Freshly ground black pepper

- 1½ lb. extra-large shrimp (26 to 30 per lb.), preferably wild, peeled and deveined
- 1½ Tbs. white-wine vinegar

Kosher salt

Position a rack in the center of the oven and heat the oven to 400°F.

Pour the oil into a 9x13-inch baking dish. Add the thyme, rosemary, and 1 tsp. pepper and bake until the oil mixture is fragrant, about 12 minutes.

Add the shrimp to the dish and toss with tongs until coated. Bake the shrimp until pink and firm, 8 to 10 minutes.

Add the vinegar and ½ tsp. salt, toss well, and let rest at room temperature until the oil cools slightly, about 5 minutes. Discard the herbs (if you choose) and serve.

salmon fillets with lemon-rosemary butter sauce

This sauce would taste good with just about anything, but it's especially delicious with salmon. **Serves 4**

- 4 **skinless salmon fillets, preferably wild (about 1½ lb.)**
  Kosher salt and freshly ground black pepper
- 2 **Tbs. olive oil, canola oil, or peanut oil**
- ¾ **cup dry white wine**
- 3 **Tbs. finely diced shallot (about 1 large)**
- 1 **tsp. chopped rosemary**
- 6 **Tbs. unsalted butter, cut into small cubes**
- 1 **tsp. fresh lemon juice**
  Kosher salt and freshly ground black pepper

Heat the oven to 425°F. Pat the salmon (or meat or chicken) thoroughly dry with paper towels. Season both sides generously with salt and pepper (about 1 tsp. of each total). Heat a 12-inch, heavy-based, ovenproof skillet over medium-high heat until a droplet of water vaporizes in 1 or 2 seconds, about 1 minute.

Add the oil, swirl it around the pan, and then evenly space the fish in the pan. Cook without touching for 2 minutes. Using tongs, lift a corner and check that the underside is both well browned and easily releases from the pan. If so, flip it over. (If not, cook for 1 to 2 more minutes before flipping.) Cook the second side for 1 minute and then transfer the skillet to the oven.

Roast until the fish reaches the doneness you want; 135°F, 4 to 7 minutes for medium.

Carefully remove the pan from the oven, transfer the fish to a large plate (don't wash the skillet), tent with foil, and let rest while you prepare the sauce.

Pour off any excess fat from the skillet. Using a large wad of paper towels, blot any remaining oil from the pan but leave any browned bits. Return the pan to high heat and add the wine, shallot, and rosemary. Cook, stirring, until the wine is almost completely evaporated, 3 to 4 minutes. Remove from the heat and whisk in the cubes of butter, adding a few at a time until they're all thoroughly incorporated and the sauce is thick and creamy looking. (If the butter is slow to melt, set the pan over low heat.) Stir in the lemon juice, season with salt and pepper to taste, and serve immediately, spooned over the salmon.

sear, roast, sauce

For the best sear, don't disturb the fish until it's had a few minutes to brown.

Finish cooking in the oven. Use an instant-read thermometer to check doneness.

Build on the browned bits in the pan to make a flavorful sauce.

roasted salmon and asparagus with lemon oil

All you need is five ingredients, and you've got a bright, springtime dish. The salmon and asparagus roast together, which makes this recipe a breeze. **Serves 4**

- 1 large lemon
- 3 Tbs. extra-virgin olive oil; more for the pan
- 20 thin stalks asparagus (10 to 12 oz.), trimmed
  Kosher salt and freshly ground black pepper
- 4 6- to 8-oz. skin-on salmon fillets, preferably wild (preferably about 1 inch thick)

Position a rack in the center of the oven and heat the oven to 450°F.

Finely grate the zest from the lemon, preferably with a rasp-style grater. In a small bowl, combine the zest with 2 Tbs. of the oil. Cut the lemon in half and set aside.

On one side of a heavy rimmed baking sheet, toss the asparagus with the remaining 1 Tbs. of the oil, ¾ tsp. salt, and ½ tsp. pepper. Spread the asparagus in one layer. Lightly coat the other side of the baking sheet with oil, and arrange the salmon fillets, skin side down, on the oiled area. Sprinkle with 1 tsp. salt and ½ tsp. pepper.

Roast until the asparagus is tender and the salmon is cooked to your liking (cut into a fillet with a paring knife to check), 10 to 13 minutes for medium. If the asparagus needs more time to cook, transfer the salmon to a platter, tent it loosely with foil, and return the asparagus to the oven until tender.

Arrange the salmon and asparagus on a platter and drizzle the lemon oil all over both. Squeeze a little juice from a lemon half over the salmon and serve immediately.

how to buy and store salmon fillets

Here's what you need to know when shopping for fresh salmon fillets:

- Wild Pacific salmon, preferably from Alaska, is a delicious, sustainable choice. There are several kinds of Pacific salmon on the market, but for the best flavor and texture look for king salmon (also known as Chinook), sockeye (red) salmon, or coho (silver) salmon.

- As with any fish, freshness is key. Try to buy fish on the day you plan to cook it, and seek out the freshest fish your market has to offer. Look for firm, moist flesh that isn't mushy or slimy. The aroma should be clean and briny, like the sea.

- Once you've selected your fillets, ask the fishmonger to scale them. Before cooking, remove any pin bones.

- At home, store the fish in a plastic bag in the coldest part of the refrigerator. If you need to store it overnight, set the fish in its plastic bag on a bed of ice in the refrigerator.

spice-rubbed and sear-roasted salmon with honey-glazed fennel

The richness of salmon is contrasted by the sweet-tart fennel salad. If you use paprika instead of sumac, the fish and fennel will take on a rich, red hue. **Serves 4**

FOR THE SPICE RUB

- **1** Tbs. coriander seeds
- **2** Tbs. ground sumac or sweet paprika
- **2** tsp. finely grated lemon zest
- **2** tsp. kosher salt

FOR THE FISH AND FENNEL

- **4** 6-oz. skinless salmon fillets, preferably wild
- **4½** tsp. freshly squeezed lemon juice
- **1** Tbs. honey
- **3** Tbs. plus 1 tsp. olive oil
- **1** small fennel bulb, quartered, cored, and sliced lengthwise about ⅜ inch thick, to yield 1½ cups (save about ½ cup of the fronds for garnish)
- **½** Granny Smith apple
  Kosher salt and freshly ground black pepper
- **½** to ¾ tsp. fennel pollen (optional)

Heat the oven to 425°F. In a small skillet, heat the coriander seeds over medium heat, stirring frequently, until they are lightly golden-brown and aromatic, about 3 minutes. Remove from the heat and let cool slightly. Grind the seeds in an electric grinder and transfer to a small bowl. Use your fingers to stir in the sumac or paprika, lemon zest, and salt.

Generously coat the salmon fillets on all sides with the rub and set the fillets on a plate.

In a small bowl, stir 4 tsp. of the lemon juice and the honey.

In a heavy 12-inch ovenproof skillet, heat 3 Tbs. of the oil over medium-high heat. When the oil is shimmering hot, arrange the salmon fillets evenly in the pan, skinned side up. Add the fennel to the pan, fitting it into the spaces around the fish.

(It will look like there's not much room, but you will be able to squeeze this amount of fennel around the fillets.) Sear for about 2 minutes, without moving; then use a slotted metal spatula to lift a piece of fish and check the color. When the fillets are nicely browned, flip them and put the pan in the oven. Roast until the salmon is barely cooked in the center, 4 to 6 minutes.

While the salmon is roasting, toss the fennel fronds in a medium bowl with the remaining 1 tsp. olive oil. Core the apple half and cut it into matchsticks. Add to the fennel fronds. Sprinkle the remaining ½ tsp. lemon juice over the apples, season with salt and pepper, and toss again.

When the salmon is cooked, remove the pan from the oven and transfer the salmon with the spatula to serving plates. Taste the fennel; if it is still crunchy, set the pan over medium heat and cook the fennel a few minutes more, stirring occasionally, until it's tender. With the spatula, transfer the fennel to a small plate.

Pour off and discard any oil in the pan, blotting the pan with a wad of paper towels (there will be some browned spice rub sticking to the pan, which is fine). Return the pan to the stove over medium-high heat and add the lemon-honey mixture. Bring to a boil, stirring with a whisk or wooden spoon to release the browned bits. Add the cooked fennel and stir to coat it with the glaze. Remove the pan from the heat. Season to taste with salt and pepper.

Top each piece of salmon with some of the glazed fennel and then a little mound of apple salad. If any glaze remains in the pan, drizzle some around each piece of salmon. Sprinkle each portion with a good pinch of fennel pollen, if using, and serve immediately.

roasted salmon with mustard and tarragon

Fresh tarragon pairs beautifully with salmon, and just a little goes a long way in this simple recipe. Round out the meal with asparagus and boiled potatoes. **Serves 6**

¼ cup mayonnaise

1 Tbs. plus 1 tsp. coarse-grained Dijon mustard

2 tsp. fresh lime juice

2 tsp. finely chopped fresh tarragon

6 6-oz. center-cut, skin-on salmon fillets, preferably wild

Kosher salt

Position a rack in the center of the oven and heat the oven to 400°F. Line a heavy-duty rimmed baking sheet with foil.

In a small bowl, stir together the mayonnaise, mustard, lime juice, and tarragon. Arrange the salmon skin side down on the baking sheet and sprinkle lightly with salt. Spread the mayonnaise mixture evenly over each fillet (there may be a little left over).

Roast the salmon until just cooked through (see Test Kitchen, p. 136, for a way to test doneness), 10 to 14 minutes. Using a spatula, lift the fillets off the baking sheet, leaving the skin behind, and transfer to plates.

Tarragon's leaves bruise easily, so go gently when chopping. Pull the leaves from the stem, then stack them and give them just a few swipes of the knife.

Rosemary-Garlic Chicken with
Apple and Fig Compote, p. 46

Poultry

Here are new flavor twists to try with ever-versatile roast chicken, plus sumptuous recipes for roasted turkey and duck.

the recipes

rosemary-garlic chicken
with apple and fig compote

Stuffing chicken breasts with minced rosemary and garlic and then tying the breasts together creates little roasts infused with flavor. For best flavor, you will need to start 1 day ahead. Serve sliced as shown on p. 44. **Serves 4**

FOR THE CHICKEN

- **3** **Tbs. fresh rosemary leaves, minced**
- **5** **medium cloves garlic, minced**
  Kosher salt and freshly ground black pepper
- **4** **bone-in, skin-on split chicken breasts**
- **1** **Tbs. canola oil**

FOR THE COMPOTE

- **1** **medium Granny Smith apple, peeled, cored, and cut into ⅓-inch pieces**
- **2** **oz. dried figs, cut into small dice (about ⅓ cup; or substitute pitted prunes)**
- **⅓** **cup red currant jelly**
- **¼** **cup dry white wine, such as Sauvignon Blanc**
- **1** **tsp. dry mustard, preferably Colman's®**
- **½** **tsp. yellow mustard seeds**
  Kosher salt and freshly ground black pepper
- **¼** **cup coarsely chopped toasted walnuts**

In a small bowl combine the rosemary, garlic, 2 tsp. salt, and ½ tsp. pepper.

Cut the chicken breasts away from the bones, leaving the skin intact. With a paring knife, cut out the white tendon on the underside of each breast.

Rub the rosemary-garlic mixture all over the chicken, including under the skin, taking care to keep the skin attached to the meat. Stack two breasts so that the skin faces outward and each breast's thicker rounded end is on top of the thinner tapered end of the other. Tie the breasts together with butcher's twine, forming a little roast. Repeat with the remaining 2 breasts. Reposition any skin that may have bunched up while tying and season the roasts all over with 1 tsp. salt and a few grinds of pepper. Put the roasts on a rack over a small baking sheet and refrigerate, uncovered, overnight.

Put the apple, figs, jelly, wine, dry mustard, mustard seeds, a generous pinch of salt, and a few grinds of pepper in a small saucepan. Bring just to a boil over medium-high heat and then reduce the heat to a gentle simmer. Cook, stirring occasionally, until the apples are tender but not mushy, about 10 minutes. Let the mixture cool to room temperature.

Let the chicken sit at room temperature for 30 minutes. Meanwhile, position a rack in the center of the oven and heat the oven to 450°F.

Heat the oil in a 10-inch skillet over medium-high heat until shimmering hot. Sear the chicken until dark golden-brown on all sides, 6 to 8 minutes total. Return the chicken to the rack over the baking sheet. Roast until a thermometer inserted in the center of each roast reads 165°F, 20 to 30 minutes. Let rest for 15 minutes. Remove the strings from the chicken and carefully slice each roast on the diagonal into ½-inch-thick medallions. Stir the toasted walnuts into the compote and serve with the chicken.

the big thaw

Many markets only sell birds like Cornish game hens frozen, so be sure to allow time for thawing. The best way to thaw poultry is in its original wrapper in the refrigerator. (Put the birds on a rimmed tray in case of any leaks.)

roasted cornish game hens with cranberry-port sauce

This is a great dish for company because much of the work, from preparing the hens to making the broth for the sauce, should be done a day ahead. **Serves 8**

FOR THE HENS

- 4   **Cornish game hens (1½ to 2 lb. each)**
- 4   **tsp. finely chopped fresh sage (stems reserved for the broth)**
- 4   **tsp. chopped fresh thyme (stems reserved for the broth)**
-     **Kosher salt and freshly ground black pepper**
- 1   **Tbs. unsalted butter**

FOR THE BROTH

- 2   **tsp. extra-virgin olive oil**
- 2   **cups lower-salt chicken broth**
- ⅓   **cup chopped shallot**

FOR THE SAUCE

- ⅓   **cup ruby port**
- ⅓   **cup dried cranberries**
- 1   **Tbs. unsalted butter**
- 1   **Tbs. minced shallot**
- 1   **Tbs. all-purpose flour**
-     **Kosher salt and freshly ground black pepper**

PREPARE THE HENS

Using poultry shears, remove the backbones from the hens by cutting along both sides. Set each hen breast side up on a cutting board and flatten by pressing down on the breastbone with your palms. With a chef's knife, split each hen in two along the breastbone. Extend the wings on each side and chop off the last two joints. Discard any large deposits of fat. Chop or break each backbone into 2 pieces and set aside with the wing tips.

In a small bowl, combine the sage and thyme with 1 Tbs. salt and 1 tsp. pepper. Pat the hens dry and rub the herb mixture on both sides of each hen. Arrange the hens skin side up on a rimmed baking sheet so they aren't touching and refrigerate, uncovered, for at least 12 hours or overnight.

MAKE THE BROTH AND START THE SAUCE

Pat the reserved wings and back bones dry. Heat the oil over medium-high heat in a 3- to 4-quart saucepan. Add the wings and back bones and cook, stirring a few times, until browned on all sides, about 8 minutes. Add the chicken broth, chopped shallot, and reserved sage and thyme stems. Simmer gently, adjusting the heat as needed, for 30 minutes. Strain, discarding the solids. Cool the broth and refrigerate overnight.

Combine the port and cranberries for the sauce in a small bowl, cover, and let sit overnight.

ROAST THE HENS

An hour before roasting, remove the hens from the refrigerator and let sit at room temperature. Position a rack in the center of the oven and heat the oven to 450°F.

Melt the 1 Tbs. butter and brush it lightly over the hens. Roast, rotating the pan about halfway though, until an instant-read thermometer inserted into the thickest part of a thigh reads 175°F to 180°F, about 30 minutes. Let rest at least 5 minutes before serving.

MAKE THE SAUCE

While the hens roast, skim the fat from the broth and heat the broth in a small saucepan. Heat the 1 Tbs. butter in a medium saucepan over medium heat. Add the minced shallot and cook, stirring occasionally, until the shallot is tender, about 2 minutes. Stir in the flour and cook, whisking gently, until it forms a thick paste, about 30 seconds. Strain the port through a fine sieve into the saucepan, reserving the cranberries (don't press down on the berries). Whisk for about 30 seconds. Slowly whisk in the broth until the sauce is smooth, adjusting the heat to maintain a steady simmer. Simmer, whisking occasionally, until reduced by about one-third, 5 to 8 minutes. Stir in the reserved cranberries. Season to taste with salt and pepper. Keep warm.

Just before serving, pour any accumulated juices from the hens into the sauce. Serve the hens drizzled with the sauce.

dry-brining and splitting

A dry brine of salt, pepper, and fresh herbs, combined with air drying the hens in the fridge overnight, helps crisp the skin during roasting. Splitting the hens in half before roasting is convenient for serving (half a hen makes a perfect single portion) but also has benefits for the cook: It's neater and eliminates any need for tableside carving; the split hens roast more quickly and evenly; and best of all, it leaves you with a pot full of backbones and wingtips that become the base for a rich sauce.

lemon-garlic roast chicken with yuzu kosho

Yuzu kosho, a spicy-tart Japanese condiment made from the zest of yuzu (an aromatic Asian fruit) combined with chiles and salt, brings bold flavor to these lemony roast chicken breasts. Yuzu kosho is very spicy, so start with a little and increase the amount as your palate permits. Serve with steamed broccoli tossed with sautéed fresh ginger, soy sauce, and sesame oil. **Serves 4**

1 **Tbs. fresh thyme leaves**

1 **medium clove garlic, peeled**
Kosher salt

4 **large, bone-in, skin-on chicken breast halves (about 3½ lb.)**

1 **large lemon, ¾ inch cut from each end and the rest thinly sliced crosswise (about 12 slices)**

2 **Tbs. canola oil**
Freshly ground black pepper

2 **to 4 tsp. green yuzu kosho**

Position a rack in the center of the oven and heat the oven to 350°F.

Mince and then smear the thyme, garlic, and a pinch of salt together with the side of a chef's knife to create a paste.

Rub the skin of the chicken breasts with the cut side of the lemon ends. Carefully loosen the skin of each breast and spread about ½ tsp. of the garlic-thyme paste between the skin and meat. Smooth the skin over the paste, brush the chicken breasts all over with the oil, and season with ½ tsp. salt and ½ tsp. pepper total.

Set a wire rack over a large rimmed baking sheet lined with foil and arrange the lemon slices in a single layer on the rack. Put the chicken breasts skin side up on the lemon slices and roast until an instant-read thermometer inserted in the thickest part of a breast registers 150°F, about 35 minutes.

Raise the oven temperature to 450°F and continue roasting until the skin is crisp and browned and the thermometer registers 165°F, about 10 minutes more. Remove from the oven. Using a pastry brush, spread the yuzu kosho in a thin layer all over the skin of the chicken. Serve the chicken with the lemon slices, if you like.

roast chicken with fingerling potatoes, leeks, and bacon

Sautéing the leeks and garlic before layering them with the potatoes renders them meltingly tender and slightly caramelized. The roast chicken on top comes out incredibly juicy, with delicate herbal notes.

Serves 4

1	3½- to 4-lb. whole chicken
	Kosher salt and freshly ground black pepper
2	Tbs. finely chopped fresh parsley, plus 10 small sprigs
4	fresh or dried bay leaves
1	Tbs. finely chopped fresh thyme, plus 4 sprigs
4	large leeks, white and light-green parts halved lengthwise, then sliced crosswise into ⅜-inch pieces (about 4 cups) and rinsed; dark-green parts from 1 leek rinsed and reserved
3	strips thick-cut bacon, cut crosswise ⅜ inch thick
1	Tbs. olive oil
2	large cloves garlic, thinly sliced
1½	lb. large fingerling potatoes, cut crosswise into ⅛-inch-thick rounds
1½	cups lower-salt chicken broth
2	Tbs. unsalted butter, softened

Discard the giblets from the chicken, trim off any excess fat from the cavity and neck, and pat dry with paper towels. Generously season the chicken inside and out with 1 Tbs. salt and ½ tsp. pepper. Stuff the cavity with the parsley sprigs, 3 of the bay leaves (if fresh, crush lightly), 2 sprigs of thyme, and the dark leek greens. Tuck the wings behind the neck of the chicken, using the wing tips to secure any loose neck skin, if necessary. Tie the legs together with string. Let rest at room temperature for 20 to 30 minutes.

Meanwhile, position a rack in the center of the oven and heat the oven to 450°F.

In a 12-inch ovenproof skillet, cook the bacon in the oil over medium-high heat, stirring occasionally, until it begins to brown, about 7 minutes. Leaving the bacon in the pan, spoon out and reserve all but 1 Tbs. fat.

Reduce the heat to medium and add the leeks, garlic, and the remaining bay leaf and thyme sprigs, and season lightly with salt and pepper. Cook, stirring occasionally, until the leeks are soft and translucent, 5 to 7 minutes. Transfer to a plate.

In the same pan, arrange half of the potatoes in an even layer, season very lightly with salt and pepper, then scatter the leek mixture over top. Layer the remaining potatoes over the leeks, and season very lightly with salt and pepper. Pour the broth over the vegetables.

Pour 1 Tbs. of the reserved bacon fat into the cavity of the chicken. Rub the softened butter over the bird's skin, and sprinkle with the chopped thyme. Set the chicken, breast side up, on the vegetables.

Roast the chicken until an instant-read thermometer inserted into the thickest part of the thigh registers 165°F to 170°F, about 1 hour.

Transfer the chicken to a platter, remove the string, cover loosely with foil, and let rest for about 15 minutes. Meanwhile, discard the thyme sprigs and bay leaf and keep the vegetables warm in the turned-off oven.

Sprinkle the potatoes with the chopped parsley, arrange them around the chicken, and serve.

turkey thighs stuffed with porcini, sausage, and artichoke hearts

Buy skin-on, bone-in thighs at the grocery store and remove the bones yourself. **Serves 6**

FOR THE STUFFING

- ¾ oz. dried porcini mushrooms (about ½ cup)
- 1 Tbs. olive oil
- ¼ lb. sweet Italian sausage, casings removed (1 link)
- 1 cup finely chopped yellow onion
- 2 tsp. minced garlic
- ½ cup coarsely chopped frozen artichoke hearts (no need to thaw)
- ½ tsp. chopped fresh thyme
- ½ tsp. chopped fresh rosemary
- ½ cup coarse day-old breadcrumbs
- ¼ cup freshly grated Parmigiano-Reggiano
   Kosher salt and freshly ground black pepper
- 1 large egg, lightly beaten

FOR THE THIGHS

- 3 turkey thighs (14 to 18 oz. each), boned (see Test Kitchen, p. 130)
   Kosher salt and freshly ground black pepper
- 2 Tbs. extra-virgin olive oil

MAKE THE STUFFING

Put the porcini in a bowl and cover with boiling water. Soak until soft, about 30 minutes. With a slotted spoon, remove the mushrooms from the liquid and chop finely. Save the liquid for another use or discard.

Heat the olive oil in a heavy-duty 10-inch skillet over medium heat. Add the sausage and cook, using the side of a metal spoon or fork to break the meat into small pieces, until browned, about 5 minutes. Add the onion and garlic and cook, stirring, until the vegetables are soft and translucent, about 3 minutes. Stir in the chopped porcini, artichokes, thyme, and rosemary and cook for 2 minutes more. Transfer the sausage mixture to a large bowl and stir in the breadcrumbs and the Parmigiano. Season to taste with salt and pepper, and then stir in the egg. Spread the mixture on a plate and chill in the freezer for 15 to 20 minutes.

STUFF THE TURKEY THIGHS

Position a rack in the center of the oven and heat the oven to 350°F.

Lightly season the boned thighs with salt and pepper. Spoon ½ to ⅔ cup of the stuffing into the empty cavity of one of the turkey thighs and spread the stuffing with the back of a spoon to fill the cavity completely. Repeat with the other thighs. Roll each thigh into a roughly cylindrical shape.

Tie each stuffed thigh with two to four loops of twine to secure. (It's OK if some of the stuffing pokes out at the ends, because the egg holds the stuffing together.) Brush the skin side of the thighs with the olive oil. Lay the thighs seam side down in a small roasting pan or heavy-duty rimmed baking sheet and roast for 30 minutes.

Brush the thighs with the pan drippings and continue to roast until the internal temperature reaches 165°F, 15 to 30 minutes more. Remove the strings and transfer the thighs to a warm platter. Let rest 10 minutes and then cut into ½-inch-thick slices and serve.

pan-roasted chicken with olives and lemon

This dish is elegant enough for entertaining but simple enough to make anytime.

Serves 4

- 1 4-lb. chicken, cut into 8 pieces
   Kosher salt and freshly ground black pepper
- 1 medium lemon
- 1 Tbs. unsalted butter; more as needed
- 1 Tbs. extra-virgin olive oil
- 5 medium shallots, peeled and quartered lengthwise
- ¾ cup jarred brined olives, rinsed, pitted, and halved
- 8 fresh sage leaves
- 6 small fresh or 3 dried bay leaves
- 2 sprigs fresh thyme, plus 1 tsp. chopped

Position a rack in the center of the oven and heat the oven to 425°F.

Season the chicken generously on all sides with salt and pepper.

Cut the ends off the lemon, stand it on one end, and slice off the peel and the bitter white pith to expose the flesh. Cut the lemon segments from the membranes, letting them drop into a small bowl. Cut each segment crosswise into 4 pieces.

Heat the butter and the oil in a 12-inch ovenproof skillet over medium-high heat. Working in batches if necessary, cook the chicken skin side down until golden-brown, 5 to 6 minutes. Transfer the chicken to a plate. Pour off all but 2 Tbs. of the fat. Add the shallots, olives, sage, bay leaves, thyme sprigs, and lemon segments, and cook until fragrant, 1 to 2 minutes.

Return the chicken to the pan skin side up and transfer to the oven. Roast until an instant-read thermometer inserted into the thickest part of a thigh registers 165°F, 18 to 20 minutes. Serve, sprinkled with the chopped thyme.

roasted turkey breast, porchetta-style

This centerpiece dish starts with a boned breast (do this yourself—see Test Kitchen, p. 130, for more information—or ask the butcher to do it for you) or two boneless breast halves. It's rubbed with a spice paste and topped with pancetta for a clever take on porchetta, a traditional Italian preparation.

Serves 7 to 9

- 1 tsp. coriander seeds
- 1 tsp. fennel seeds
- 1 Tbs. chopped fresh rosemary
- 2 tsp. chopped fresh sage
- 3 medium cloves garlic
   Kosher salt and freshly ground black pepper
- 3 Tbs. olive oil
- 1 whole skin-on turkey breast (5 to 7 lb.), boned (see Test Kitchen, p. 130) or 2 boneless skin-on turkey breast halves (2 to 3 lb. each)
- 8 ⅛-inch-thick pancetta slices, unrolled into strips, or 8 strips thick-cut bacon

In a large mortar, pound the coriander and fennel seeds with a pestle to form a coarse powder. Add the rosemary and sage and pound to crush and bruise the herbs. Add the garlic and 1 Tbs. salt and pound until a paste begins to form. Stir in 2 tsp. pepper and 2 Tbs. of the olive oil and set aside.

Pat the turkey breast dry with a paper towel and lay it skin side down on a work surface. Rub half the spice paste over the meat. Turn the turkey over and carefully separate the skin from the meat without tearing the skin. Rub the remaining spice paste under the skin. Reform the breast and tie with 4 to 6 loops of butcher's twine to make a roll. (If you're using boneless halves, season the two halves, lay them on top of each other skin side out, and tie them together.) Wrap in plastic and refrigerate for at least 2 hours and up to 24 hours.

Position a rack in the center of the oven and heat the oven to 350°F.

Heat the remaining 1 Tbs. oil in a 12-inch skillet over medium heat. Add the turkey breast and cook until golden-brown on all sides, about 5 minutes total. Transfer the breast seam side down to a roasting pan fitted with a rack. Crisscross the pancetta over the top of the breast. Roast until the internal temperature reaches 165°F on an instant-read thermometer, 1¼ to 1½ hours. Let the turkey breast rest for 15 to 20 minutes.

Remove the pancetta and chop or crumble it. Remove the strings from the turkey, slice into ¼-inch slices, and serve, sprinkled with the pancetta.

butter-and-herb-roasted turkey with madeira jus

Butter, garlic, and fresh herbs flavor this juicy roasted turkey. A Madeira jus, made from homemade turkey broth and the pan drippings, is quicker to make than traditional gravy and just as delicious. **Serves 10 to 12, with a good probability of leftovers**

FOR THE BROTH

- 3 Tbs. extra-virgin olive oil
- Neck from a 13- to 14-lb. turkey, cut into 3 or 4 pieces
- Giblets from a 13- to 14-lb. turkey, chopped (optional)
- Sea salt
- 4 medium cloves garlic, chopped
- 2 medium carrots, chopped
- 2 large celery stalks, chopped
- 1 large yellow onion, chopped
- 1 dried bay leaf
- 3 to 4 sprigs fresh flat-leaf parsley
- 2 to 3 fresh sage leaves
- 1 small sprig fresh rosemary
- 2 to 3 cups lower-salt chicken broth
- 1 cup Madeira

FOR THE TURKEY

- 1 13- to 14-lb. turkey (preferably fresh; not kosher or self-basting)
- ½ medium lemon
- Sea salt

- 1 medium head garlic, separated into cloves and peeled
- ½ cup unsalted butter, softened
- 1 Tbs. finely chopped fresh thyme
- Freshly ground black pepper
- 4 sprigs fresh sage (7 to 8 inches long)
- 4 sprigs fresh rosemary (6 to 7 inches long)
- ⅓ cup celery leaves (optional)

MAKE THE BROTH

Heat 2 Tbs. of the oil in a 10-inch straight-sided skillet over medium-high heat. Cook the neck and giblets (if using) with a pinch of salt, stirring often, until browned, 9 to 10 minutes .

Transfer the neck and giblets to a bowl. Heat the remaining 1 Tbs. oil and add the garlic, carrots, celery, onion, bay leaf, and a big pinch of salt. Cook, stirring often, until browned, 8 to 9 minutes **1**.

Return the neck and giblets to the skillet. Add the parsley, sage, and rosemary. Add

1½ cups of water, 2 cups of the broth, and the Madeira. Bring to a boil; then reduce the heat and simmer, partially covered, until intensely flavorful, about 2½ hours. If the liquid level drops enough to expose the solids, add more broth.

Strain the broth through a fine sieve into a large bowl — you'll have 2 to 2½ cups.

ROAST THE TURKEY

Position a rack in the bottom of the oven and heat the oven to 325°F. Put a V-rack in a large roasting pan.

Rinse and dry the turkey. Rub the inside of the body and neck cavities with the cut side of the lemon half, and sprinkle 1 tsp. salt inside the cavities.

Thinly slice 3 garlic cloves. Carefully slide your hands under the skin of the turkey to loosen it from the breast. Push the garlic slices between the skin and the breast, being careful not to tear the skin **2**.

Mix the butter with the thyme, 2 tsp. salt, and a few grinds of pepper in a small bowl. Spread half of the butter inside the body cavity of the turkey. Put the lemon half, 3 sage sprigs, 3 rosemary sprigs, the celery leaves (if using), and about three-quarters

continued on p. 56

a glorious bird, step by step

Brown the broth ingredients well. The caramelization will lend deep flavor to the finished broth.

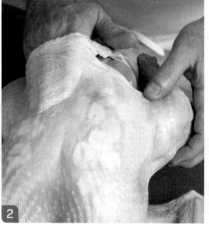

To infuse the turkey with flavor as it roasts, push slices of fresh garlic between the skin and breast. Go slowly to avoid tearing the skin.

Stuff the turkey with thyme butter, a lemon half, garlic cloves, and fresh herb sprigs to perfume the bird from the inside out.

> **Make Ahead**
>
> The broth for the Madeira jus — before the turkey drippings are added — may be prepared 2 days ahead and refrigerated in an airtight container. After roasting, the turkey can rest at room temperature for up to 1 hour. Reheat the broth before making the jus.

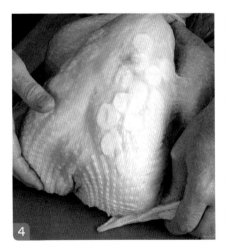

4

Tuck the wing tips behind the neck like this so they don't burn during roasting. If there's any loose skin around the neck, use the wing tips to secure it in place over the neck cavity.

5

Spread thyme butter over the turkey to help the skin brown and to up the flavor quotient. Don't worry about indentations left by the rack— they'll diminish before the bird is done.

6

Check for doneness by inserting an instant-read thermometer into the thickest part of both thighs. Avoid touching bone, or the reading will be off. You want a temperature between 170°F and 175°F.

continued from p. 54

of the remaining garlic cloves in the cavity **3**. Put the remaining herb sprigs and garlic cloves in the neck cavity.

Tie the legs together for a neater appearance, if you like. Tuck the wing tips behind the neck **4**, securing any loose skin over the neck cavity beneath the wing tips. Set the turkey in the V-rack, breast side down. Rub half of the remaining thyme butter over the back of the turkey and sprinkle with salt. Roast for 1 hour.

Remove the pan from the oven and baste the turkey with the pan drippings. With silicone oven mitts or two wads of paper towels, flip the turkey onto its back. Spread the remaining thyme butter over the breast and legs **5**, sprinkle with salt, and roast for 1 hour more.

Baste and continue to roast for 30 minutes more. Baste again and then check the temperature by placing an instant-read thermometer in the thickest part of both thighs **6**. The turkey is done when the thermometer registers 170°F to 175°F and the juices run clear when the thermometer is removed. If necessary, continue roasting and checking the temperature every 10 minutes. If at any time the turkey gets too dark on top, tent it loosely with foil.

Remove the pan from the oven. With silicone oven mitts or wads of paper towels, tilt the turkey so the juices in the cavity run into the roasting pan. Transfer the turkey to a serving platter or cutting board and tent it loosely with foil. Reserve the drippings in the roasting pan. Let the turkey rest for at least 30 minutes and up to 1 hour before carving.

MAKE THE JUS

Strain the drippings from the roasting pan through a fine sieve into the Madeira broth. Transfer to a fat separator, wait until the fat has risen to the top, and then slowly separate the broth from the fat into a clean 2-quart saucepan. Discard the fat.

Bring the sauce to a simmer over medium heat and season to taste with salt and pepper. If the jus is too concentrated and salty, add a little water.

Carve the turkey and serve with the jus.

plum-glazed duck breasts

The elegance of this dish belies its simplicity. The secret is the sweet spiced glaze, made with plum preserves and Asian seasonings. If you can't find plum preserves, cherry or currant preserves make good substitutes. **Serves 4**

2	boneless, skin-on duck breast halves (about 1 lb. each)
	Kosher salt and freshly ground black pepper
½	cup plum preserves
1	Tbs. reduced-sodium soy sauce
¼	tsp. Chinese five-spice powder
	Pinch crushed red pepper flakes
3	scallions, thinly sliced

Position a rack in the center of the oven and heat the oven to 425°F. Trim any excess skin and fat from the duck and score the remaining skin and fat underneath in a 1-inch diamond pattern, taking care not to cut the flesh. Pat the duck dry and season generously with salt and pepper.

Heat a 12-inch heavy-duty skillet over medium-high heat. Put the duck in the skillet skin side down, reduce the heat to medium low, and render the fat until only a thin, crisp layer of skin remains, about 8 minutes.

Meanwhile, in a small bowl, combine the preserves, soy sauce, five-spice powder, and red pepper flakes.

Turn the duck over, carefully spoon off most of the fat from the skillet, and brush the preserves mixture over the breasts.

Transfer the skillet to the oven and roast until an instant-read thermometer inserted into the thickest part of a breast registers 135°F for medium rare, 8 to 10 minutes. Transfer the duck to a cutting board and let rest for 5 minutes.

Meanwhile, tilt the skillet and spoon off as much fat from the pan juice as possible. Slice the duck diagonally into ¼-inch slices. Arrange on plates and spoon the pan juice over. Sprinkle with the scallions and serve.

duck doneness

Duck breasts are best served medium rare so they stay juicy and tender, but feel free to adjust the cooking time to achieve your preferred doneness.

fresh herb- and salt-rubbed roasted turkey

A dry brine (an herb and salt rub applied directly to the turkey) creates satiny leg meat and juicy, perfectly seasoned breast meat. Air-drying the turkey on the last day of the 4-day process will make its skin super crisp when roasted. This recipe can be adapted to turkeys of all sizes— use ⅛ oz. of kosher salt per pound. **Serves 8 to 10**

- 2 **Tbs. chopped fresh thyme**
- 2 **Tbs. chopped fresh sage**
- 2 **tsp. chopped fresh rosemary**
- 1 **Tbs. extra-virgin olive oil**
- 1 **16-lb. turkey, preferably fresh (not kosher or self-basting)**
- 2 **oz. kosher salt (½ cup if using Diamond Cyrstal®; ¼ cup if using Morton®)**

  Gravy (optional)

DRY-BRINE THE TURKEY

Four days before you plan to roast the turkey, mix the herbs and oil in a small bowl. Loosen the skin around the shoulders of the bird and around the cavity. Carefully slide your hands underneath the skin to loosen it from the breast, thighs, and drumsticks.

Rub the herb mixture on the meat, under the skin. Pat the skin back into place.

Rub the salt inside the cavity and on the skin. Tuck the wing tips behind the neck and tie the legs together with kitchen string. Put the turkey in a large food-safe plastic bag (such as a turkey-size roasting bag) and tie. Put the bag inside a second bag and tie.

Refrigerate the turkey, turning it over every day, for 3 days.

Remove the turkey from the bags and pat dry. Put it in a flameproof roasting pan and refrigerate, unwrapped, to let the turkey air-dry overnight (for the fourth day).

ROAST THE TURKEY

Position a rack in the bottom third of the oven and heat the oven to 425°F. Roast the turkey for 30 minutes; then reduce the heat to 325°F. Continue to roast until an instant-read thermometer registers 170°F in the thickest part of a thigh, about 2 hours. Let the turkey rest for 30 minutes before carving to allow the juices to settle. If making gravy, do so while the turkey rests. Carve and serve.

roast chicken breasts with rosemary-lemon brown butter

Utterly simple to prepare and impossible to resist, this dish is sure to become a family favorite. Serve with brown rice and green beans or asparagus, all of which would benefit from the nutty-lemony flavor of the sauce. **Serves 4**

- 4 bone-in skin-on split chicken breasts (about 1¾ lb.)
  Kosher salt and pepper
- 1 Tbs. vegetable oil
- 4 Tbs. unsalted butter
- 1 Tbs. chopped fresh rosemary
- 1½ tsp. fresh lemon juice
  Lemon wedges, for serving

Position a rack in the center of the oven and heat the oven to 400°F.

Pat the chicken dry and generously season with salt and pepper. Heat the oil in a 12-inch ovenproof skillet over medium-high heat until shimmering hot. Add the chicken skin side down and cook until golden-brown, about 3 minutes. Turn the chicken over, transfer the pan to the oven, and roast until the chicken is cooked through (165°F), about 20 minutes. Transfer to a platter.

Pour off any fat from the skillet, add the butter, and melt over medium heat. Add the rosemary and cook, stirring, until the butter turns brown and gives off a nutty aroma, 2 to 3 minutes. Immediately remove the pan from the heat, stir in the lemon juice, and season to taste with salt and pepper. Pour the sauce over the chicken and serve with the lemon wedges.

maple-glazed roast chicken

A long soak in a sweet, slightly spicy brine makes this chicken one of the juiciest you'll ever make, infused throughout with warm maple flavor. Glazing with maple syrup makes it a showstopping, glossy-skinned beauty. **Serves 4**

- 2 cups grade B pure maple syrup
- 1 Tbs. chopped fresh sage leaves
- 1 cinnamon stick
- 1 tsp. crushed red pepper flakes
- 4 oz. kosher salt (¾ cup if using Diamond Crystal; ⅓ cup if using Morton)
- 1 3½- to 4-lb. whole chicken, giblets and excess fat removed

Combine the maple syrup, sage, cinnamon, and red pepper flakes in a 1- to 2-quart saucepan. Warm over medium-low heat to meld the flavors, about 5 minutes.

In a plastic tub or pot just large enough to submerge the chicken, combine the salt and 3 quarts cool water. Reserve ½ cup of the maple syrup mixture for the glaze, and add the rest to the water. Stir until the salt is dissolved, and let cool to room temperature. Add the chicken, breast side down, cover, and refrigerate for 8 to 24 hours.

Remove the chicken from the brine, and discard the brine. Tie the legs together with twine, fold the wings under the back, and place breast side up on a rack set in a roasting pan. Refrigerate uncovered for 1 hour to allow the skin to dry.

Position a rack in the center of the oven and heat the oven to 375°F.

Meanwhile, remove the chicken from the refrigerator and let it sit at room temperature for 30 minutes.

Roast for 10 minutes. Reduce the oven temperature to 325°F and roast for another 30 minutes. Put a cup of water in the roasting pan to prevent the syrup from burning, brush the chicken with some of the reserved maple syrup mixture, and return it to the oven, rotating the pan. Continue to roast, brushing with the maple syrup mixture every 15 minutes, until an instant-read thermometer inserted into the thickest part of the thigh reads 165°F, 35 to 45 minutes more. Let rest for 15 minutes before carving and serving.

roast chicken with chanterelles and peas

Golden roast chicken over a rich, creamy sauce of chanterelles, sweet peas, and shallots makes for a dish that's both elegant and comforting. Serve with egg noodles. **Serves 4**

3	**Tbs. olive oil**
1½	**Tbs. sherry vinegar**
1½	**Tbs. fresh lemon juice**
5	**medium garlic cloves, minced (about 5 tsp.)**
1	**3½- to 4-lb. chicken, quartered**
	Kosher salt and freshly ground black pepper

4	**Tbs. unsalted butter**
1	**cup thinly sliced shallot**
¾	**lb. fresh chanterelles (about 5 cups), cleaned, root ends trimmed, torn into bite-size pieces if large**
½	**cup dry white wine**
1	**cup heavy cream**
1	**cup frozen peas, thawed**
1	**Tbs. chopped fresh tarragon**

Position a rack in the center of the oven and heat the oven to 450°F.

Whisk the olive oil, vinegar, lemon juice, and 2 tsp. of the garlic in a large shallow bowl. Add the chicken, turn to coat, and let sit at room temperature, turning occasionally, for 30 minutes.

Put the chicken skin side up on a rack set over a large rimmed baking sheet (reserve the marinade). Season well with salt and pepper. Roast for 10 minutes, lower the heat to 375°F, and roast until the skin is deep golden and the meat is cooked through (165°F), about 30 minutes more.

Meanwhile, melt the butter in a 12-inch heavy-duty skillet over medium heat. Add the reserved marinade and the shallots. Cook, stirring, until tender and lightly browned, 3 to 4 minutes.

Add the chanterelles and cook, stirring frequently, until tender and golden-brown on some sides, about 3 minutes. Add the remaining garlic and cook, stirring, until fragrant, about 1 minute. Add the wine and simmer for 1 minute. Remove from the heat. Set aside ½ cup of the mushrooms and cover to keep warm.

Transfer the chicken to a plate, reserving the juice in the baking sheet and scraping up any browned bits. Put the skillet with the mushroom mixture over medium-high heat and add the chicken drippings, cream, peas, ¾ tsp. salt, and ½ tsp. pepper. Cook until thickened to a sauce consistency, about 2 minutes. Remove from the heat, add 2 tsp. of the tarragon, and season to taste with salt and pepper. Divide the sauce among four shallow bowls and top with the chicken. Sprinkle with the reserved mushrooms and the remaining tarragon, and serve.

mediterranean chicken with mushrooms & zucchini

Red pearl onions add nice color to this dish, but you can substitute white or yellow pearl onions or even thawed frozen ones. **Serves 4 to 6**

- 3 **Tbs. balsamic vinegar**
- 1 **Tbs. plus 1 tsp. finely chopped fresh rosemary**
- 1 **tsp. firmly packed light brown sugar**
  Kosher salt and freshly ground black pepper
- 2 **Tbs. extra-virgin olive oil**
- 1½ **cups peeled red pearl onions (6 to 7 oz.), halved if large (see Test Kitchen, p. 136, for more information)**
- 8 **oz. cremini (baby bella) mushrooms, stems trimmed**
- 2 **oz. pancetta, cut into ½-inch dice (about ⅓ cup)**
- 1 **4-lb. chicken, cut into 8 serving pieces, trimmed of extra skin and fat, patted dry**
- 2 **small zucchini (4 to 5 oz. each), trimmed, cut in half lengthwise and then crosswise into ½-inch-thick half-rounds**
- ½ **cup medium- to full-bodied red wine, such as Merlot or Syrah**

Position a rack in the center of the oven and heat the oven to 400°F.

In a small bowl, mix 1 Tbs. of the balsamic vinegar, 1 Tbs. of the rosemary, the brown sugar, ¾ tsp. salt, and ¼ tsp. pepper; stir to dissolve the sugar and salt. Add the olive oil and mix well.

Scatter the pearl onions over the bottom of a metal, glass, or ceramic baking dish that measures about 10x15x2 inches. Add the mushrooms, cap side up. Stir the vinegar mixture to mix well; spoon 1 Tbs. into a second small bowl and reserve. Use about half of the remaining mixture to brush the mushroom caps. Scatter the pancetta over the mushrooms and onions. Arrange the chicken pieces, skin side up, on top of all, and brush with the remaining vinegar mixture. Roast for 30 minutes.

Meanwhile, toss the zucchini with the reserved 1 Tbs. of the vinegar mixture. In a measuring cup, combine the wine with the remaining 2 Tbs. balsamic vinegar, 1 tsp. rosemary, and ¼ teaspoon salt. Remove the roasting pan from the oven and reduce the temperature to 375°F. Pour the

wine mixture around the chicken and then scatter the zucchini around the chicken, keeping it toward the edges of the pan as much as possible. Return the pan to the oven and continue to roast until the vegetables are tender and an instant-read thermometer registers 165°F in several pieces of chicken, 20 to 30 minutes.

Transfer the chicken to a warmed platter. With a slotted spoon, arrange the vegetables and pancetta around the chicken. Sprinkle the vegetables with a little salt.

Tilt the roasting pan so that the juices gather in one corner. With a large, shallow spoon, skim as much fat as possible from the pan sauce. Spoon a small amount of sauce over the chicken and vegetables. Put the remaining sauce in a pitcher to pass at the table.

pomegranate-orange chicken

Pomegranate and orange juices form the basis for this dynamite chicken dish that echoes eastern Mediterranean flavor combinations.

Serves 4 to 6

- 1 large orange, zest finely grated, juiced
- 1 cup pomegranate juice
- 1½ tsp. dried thyme leaves
- ⅛ tsp. ground cinnamon
  Freshly ground black pepper
- 6 tsp. canola oil
  Kosher salt
- ¾ cup lower-salt chicken broth
- 2 sweet potatoes, peeled and cut into 1-inch pieces
- 2 medium parsnips, peeled and sliced on the diagonal ¼ inch thick
- 1 red onion, peeled and cut into ¾-inch-thick wedges
- 1 4-lb. chicken, cut into 8 serving pieces, trimmed of extra skin and fat, patted dry
- 1 cup coarsely chopped walnuts

Position a rack in the center of the oven and heat the oven to 400°F.

In a medium saucepan, combine the orange juice and pomegranate juice. Bring to a boil over medium heat and reduce to ¼ cup, about 15 minutes. Add ½ tsp. of the thyme, the cinnamon, and ¼ tsp. pepper. Divide the mixture between two small bowls. To one bowl add 2 tsp. of the oil and ½ tsp. salt. To the other add the chicken broth, all but 1 tsp. of the orange zest, and ¼ tsp. salt.

Scatter the sweet potatoes, parsnips, and onion over the bottom of a metal, glass, or ceramic baking dish that measures about 10x15x2 inches. Toss with the remaining 4 tsp. of oil and 1 tsp. thyme. Arrange the chicken pieces, skin side up, on top of the vegetables and brush with all of the juice-oil mixture. Roast for 30 minutes.

Remove the pan from the oven and reduce the temperature to 375°F. Pour the juice-broth mixture around the chicken pieces and scatter the walnuts around the chicken. Return the pan to the oven and roast until the vegetables are tender and an instant-read thermometer registers 165°F in several pieces of chicken, 20 to 30 minutes.

Transfer the chicken to a warmed platter. Use a slotted spoon to arrange the vegetables and walnuts around the chicken. Sprinkle the vegetables with a little salt and sprinkle the remaining orange zest over all. Tilt the roasting pan so that the juices gather in one corner. With a large, shallow spoon, skim as much fat as possible from the pan sauce. Season the sauce to taste with salt and pepper and pour into a pitcher to pass at the table.

chicken with apples & cider

A take on the classic Norman combination of chicken, apples, and cream, this roasted version adds mustard and tarragon for extra depth, plus carrots, fennel, and onion for a one-dish meal. **Serves 4 to 6**

½ cup plus 2 Tbs. hard apple cider

2 Tbs. Dijon mustard

1 Tbs. plus 1 tsp. chopped fresh tarragon

1 Tbs. chopped fresh parsley

1 Tbs. melted unsalted butter

Kosher salt and freshly ground black pepper

2 medium carrots, peeled and sliced on the diagonal ¼ inch thick

1 small fennel bulb, trimmed, quartered, and cut lengthwise through the core into ½-inch-thick wedges

1 large yellow onion, cut into medium dice

1 14-lb. chicken, cut into 8 serving pieces, trimmed of extra skin and fat, patted dry

¼ cup crème fraîche

1 tsp. cornstarch

½ cup lower-salt chicken broth

1 tsp. cider vinegar

1 large Granny Smith apple (unpeeled), cored and cut into ½-inch pieces

1 large Braeburn apple (unpeeled), cored and cut into ½-inch pieces

Position a rack in the center of the oven and heat the oven to 400°F.

In a small bowl, mix 2 Tbs. of the cider, 1 Tbs. of the mustard, 1 Tbs. of the tarragon, 2 tsp. of the parsley, the butter, ½ tsp. salt, and ⅛ tsp. pepper.

Scatter the carrots, fennel, and onion over the bottom of a metal, glass, or ceramic baking dish that measures about 10x15x2 inches. Arrange the chicken pieces, skin side up, on top of the vegetables. Brush the cider-mustard mixture over the chicken pieces and roast for 30 minutes.

Meanwhile, in a small bowl whisk the remaining ½ cup cider, 1 Tbs. mustard, the crème fraîche, and cornstarch. Whisk in the chicken broth, vinegar, and ½ tsp. salt.

Remove the pan from the oven and reduce the temperature to 375°F. Pour the crème fraîche mixture around the chicken and then scatter the apples around. Return the pan to the oven and roast until the vegetables and apples are tender and an instant-read thermometer registers 165°F in several pieces of chicken, 20 to 30 minutes.

Transfer the chicken to a warmed platter. Use a slotted spoon to arrange the vegetables and apples around the chicken. Sprinkle with a little salt and the remaining 1 tsp. tarragon and 1 tsp. parsley. Tilt the roasting pan so that the juices gather in one corner. With a large, shallow spoon, skim as much fat as possible from the pan sauce. Season the sauce to taste with salt and pepper and pour into a pitcher to pass at the table.

Positioning the breasts in the center of the pan helps ensure the chicken pieces will be done at the same time.

citrus-marinated roasted chicken

This recipe uses a two-part roasting method: first, the chicken is roasted at a high temperature to brown the skin, and then at a lower temperature to gently cook the meat through. You can refrigerate the leftovers for up to 4 days. Store the chicken, pan juice, and citrus wedges separately. **Serves 6**

- ¼ cup extra-virgin olive oil
- 2 4-lb. whole chickens, each cut into 6 pieces (4 breasts with rib bones, 4 leg-thigh pieces, 4 wings)
- 4 large lemons
- 2 large oranges
- 8 medium cloves garlic, chopped
- 3 Tbs. chopped fresh oregano (or 1 Tbs. dried, crumbled)
- 3 Tbs. soy sauce
- 1 Tbs. honey
- ½ tsp. crushed red pepper flakes
  Kosher salt and freshly ground black pepper

Pour the olive oil into a heavy-duty nonreactive roasting pan large enough to accommodate the chicken pieces in one layer. Arrange the chicken in the pan with the breasts in the center and the legs and wings around the edge.

Cut 1 of the lemons into 6 wedges. Finely grate the zest from another lemon to yield 1 tsp. and then squeeze the remaining lemons to yield ⅔ cup juice; transfer the zest and juice to a small bowl. Cut 1 of the oranges into 8 wedges. Finely grate the zest from the remaining orange to yield 1 tsp., and then squeeze the orange to yield ½ cup juice; add to the bowl with the lemon juice and zest. Scatter the lemon and orange wedges around the chicken pieces, but don't put them on top of the chicken or they'll interfere with browning.

Stir the garlic, oregano, soy sauce, honey, and pepper flakes into the citrus juice. Pour the marinade evenly over the chicken. Cover with plastic and refrigerate, turning the chicken pieces occasionally, for at least 6 hours and up to 12 hours.

Position a rack in the center of the oven and heat the oven to 425°F.

Turn the chicken so all the pieces are skin side up. Sprinkle with 1 tsp. salt and ½ tsp. pepper. Roast for 20 minutes, and then reduce the heat to 375°F and continue to roast until the chicken is golden-brown and cooked through, about 30 minutes.

Transfer the chicken and the lemon and orange wedges to a platter. Pour the pan juice into a fat separator and let sit until the fat rises to the top. Discard the excess fat and pour the juice into a 10-inch skillet. Boil over medium-high heat until reduced to 1½ cups, about 10 minutes.

Serve the chicken with the citrus wedges, passing the reduced pan juice at the table.

roasted duck with tangerine-hoisin glaze

Rubbing the ducks with a mix of garlic, tangerine zest, five-spice powder, and coriander and then refrigerating for a day or two adds flavor and helps the skin crisp during roasting.

Serves 8

FOR THE DUCKS

- 4 medium cloves garlic, minced
- 4 tsp. finely grated tangerine zest
- 2½ tsp. coriander seed
- 2½ tsp. five-spice powder

Kosher salt and freshly ground white pepper

- 2 Pekin (Long Island) ducks (5 to 6 lb. each), giblets discarded

FOR THE GLAZE

- 3 Tbs. hoisin sauce
- 2 Tbs. orange liqueur, such as Grand Marnier® or Triple Sec
- 1 Tbs. honey
- 1 Tbs. fresh tangerine juice
- 1 tsp. Asian sesame oil

SEASON THE DUCKS

In a mortar or spice grinder, grind the garlic, tangerine zest, coriander, five-spice, 2 Tbs. salt, and 1 tsp. pepper to a coarse paste. **Make 20 to 30** small slits in the skin of each duck, using a sharp paring knife held parallel to the duck surface so that you pierce the skin and fat but not the meat. Be sure to make slits on the backs and thighs as well as the breasts. Rub about two-thirds of the spice mixture into the duck cavities and then rub the remaining all over the skin. Set the ducks on a rack over a large rimmed baking sheet and allow to air dry uncovered in the refrigerator for 24 to 36 hours.

ROAST THE DUCKS

Position a rack in the center of the oven and heat the oven to 325°F. Let the ducks sit at room temperature as the oven heats. Arrange the ducks breast down on two small V-racks in a large roasting pan and roast for 1¼ hours. Remove the pan from the oven and spoon or pour off most of the fat from the roasting pan—use a turkey baster if you have one. Flip the ducks, using sturdy tongs inserted in the cavities, and pierce the skin again all over with a knife. Continue roasting the ducks until the meat around the thighs feels tender when prodded (a skewer should penetrate the thigh with no resistance), the legs feel loose in their joints, and an instant-read thermometer inserted in the thickest part of the thigh near the joint reads 175°F, 45 to 60 minutes more.

GLAZE THE DUCKS

Remove the ducks from the oven, and increase the oven temperature to 500°F. In a small bowl, whisk the hoisin, orange liqueur, honey, tangerine juice, and sesame oil. Transfer the ducks (on the racks) to a rimmed baking sheet. With a brush, paint the breasts and legs with a thin layer of glaze and return to the oven. Paint again after 5 minutes and continue roasting until mahogany-color, 3 to 5 minutes more. **Let the ducks rest** for 5 to 10 minutes before carving.

slow-roasting

Roasting the duck slowly at a low temperature (breast side down first) is the best way to render the fat from under the breast skin. It's key to remove the rendered fat from the pan partway through roasting, so the duck won't sit in its own fat as it finishes roasting, which would prevent it from crisping.

five-spice powder

A warm and fragrant spice blend common in Chinese cuisine, five-spice powder is typically composed of star anise, cloves, fennel seed, cinnamon, and Sichuan peppercorns. Licorice root and ginger are also components of some recipes. It's available at most supermarkets.

roasted goose with brandied prune stuffing and red-wine gravy

If you have an oval roaster with a cover, this is an ideal time to use it. For a special occasion, consider a goose, which becomes tender and succulent with crisp, browned skin after steam-roasting. You'll need to prepare the goose, make the broth, and prepare the bread and prunes a day ahead. **Serves 8 to 10**

FOR THE GOOSE

- 1   12- to 14-lb. goose (with giblets)
  Kosher salt and freshly ground black pepper

FOR THE BROTH

- 1   Tbs. peanut or vegetable oil
- 1   medium yellow onion, coarsely chopped
- 1   medium carrot, coarsely chopped
- 1   medium celery stalk, coarsely chopped
- 2   fresh thyme sprigs
- 1   dried bay leaf
  Kosher salt

FOR THE STUFFING

- 1   cup prunes, chopped into ⅓-inch pieces
- 2   Tbs. brandy
- 5   cups lightly packed ¾-inch bread cubes (from a loaf of French or Italian bread)
- 2   cups chopped celery, including leaves (about 4 stalks)
- 1¾   cups chopped yellow onion (1 large)
- 2   medium cloves garlic, minced
  Kosher salt and freshly ground black pepper
- 1   Tbs. fresh thyme leaves, lightly chopped
- ½   cup chopped fresh flat-leaf parsley
- 1   tsp. finely grated orange zest
- 1   tsp. finely grated lemon zest

FOR THE GRAVY

- ¾   cup dry red wine, such as Cabernet Sauvignon or Shiraz/Syrah
- 2   Tbs. all-purpose flour
- 2   Tbs. currant or plum jelly
  Kosher salt and freshly ground black pepper

PREPARE THE GOOSE

Pull the giblets out of the cavity. Refrigerate the liver for use in the stuffing and set the other giblets aside for the broth. Tear off any loose deposits of fat from inside the cavity openings. With a chef's knife, cut off and reserve the two long outermost sections of each wing, leaving only the section nearest the breast still attached. Next, with a paring knife, prick holes in the skin around the thighs, being careful not to cut into the meat. Finally, season the goose generously inside and out with salt and pepper. Set on a rack on a baking sheet and refrigerate, uncovered, overnight.

MAKE THE BROTH AND START THE STUFFING

Using a cleaver, chop the neck and wings into 4-inch sections. Pat dry with paper towels. Heat the oil in a 5-quart soup pot over medium heat. Add the neck, wings, and giblets (excluding the liver). Cook, turning occasionally, until browned on all sides, 10 to 15 minutes. Add the onion, carrot, celery, thyme, and bay leaf and stir. Add 1 quart water and a small pinch of salt and bring to a boil. Immediately reduce the heat to medium low and simmer gently for 2 hours. Strain, discarding the solids, and cool to room temperature before refrigerating. You should have 1⅓ to 1¾ cups broth.

Combine the prunes and brandy for the stuffing in a small bowl, cover, and steep overnight. Arrange the bread cubes for the stuffing on a baking sheet and set aside, uncovered, to dry overnight.

STEAM THE GOOSE

Put the goose breast side up on a V-rack in a large flameproof roasting pan with sides at least 3 inches high. Set the pan on the top of the stove over the largest burner and add about 1 inch of water. Cover the roasting pan tightly with heavy-duty foil (or with the domed lid if using a covered roaster). Bring to a boil and lower the heat so the water just simmers. Steam the goose for 40 minutes. Check the liquid occasionally to make sure it hasn't evaporated and add hot water if necessary. Turn off the heat and uncover the pan, being careful of the steam. Remove the goose and rack from the pan and set aside for 20 to 30 minutes until cool enough to handle.

MAKE THE STUFFING AND ROAST THE GOOSE

Position a rack in the center of the oven and heat the oven to 325°F. Spoon 2 Tbs. rendered goose fat from the steaming liquid in the roasting pan (reserving the rest) and put it in a medium skillet over medium heat. Add the goose liver and sauté, turning a few times, until it browns and feels springy, about 6 minutes. Transfer to a cutting board to cool. Return the skillet to medium heat and add the celery, onion, garlic, thyme, and ½ tsp. each salt and pepper. Stir, cover, and reduce the heat to medium low. Cook, stirring occasionally, until the vegetables are soft, 10 to 12 minutes.

Transfer the vegetables to a large mixing bowl. Stir in the bread cubes, soaked prunes, parsley, orange and lemon zests, and ½ tsp. salt. Chop the liver and add it to the bowl.

Check the goose for pinfeathers or quills—these are most often found around the legs. Remove any with strong tweezers or pliers.

Using a large spoon, loosely fill the large cavity of the goose with stuffing. If there is any leftover stuffing, use it to fill the smaller neck cavity.

Pour the steaming liquid from the roasting pan into a clean vessel and leave at room temperature until cool. When the liquid and fat are cool enough to handle, spoon the fat off, set aside 2 Tbs. for the gravy, and reserve the rest for future use (see Test Kitchen, p. 134); discard the water.

Return the roasting rack and goose to the roasting pan. Roast for 1½ hours and then rotate the pan for even cooking. Continue roasting until the meat on the drumsticks feels very soft when pressed, ½ to 1 hour more. You can also check that the thigh (near the joint) is 175°F to 180°F and that the stuffing is at least 165°F. Remove the goose from the oven.

Set the goose in a draft-free spot to rest for 20 to 45 minutes. If the kitchen is cool, tent the bird loosely with foil.

MAKE THE GRAVY

Pour off the fat from the roasting pan, being careful to leave behind all the tasty pan drippings. Set the roasting pan over medium heat on the largest burner and add the wine, stirring and scraping with a wooden spoon to loosen all the pan drippings. Bring to a boil and reduce by about half, stirring often, about 3 minutes. Scrape the contents of the roasting pan into a strainer set over a bowl.

In a medium saucepan over medium heat, heat the 2 Tbs. reserved goose fat. Whisk in the flour and continue whisking for about 1 minute. Slowly whisk in the liquid from the roasting pan and then whisk in the broth. Simmer, whisking frequently, until thickened and full-flavored, about 5 minutes. Whisk in the jelly until melted. Season to taste with salt and pepper, and keep warm while you carve the goose.

Serve the goose and stuffing with the gravy on the side.

steam-roasting

This combination cooking method involves steaming on the stovetop and then slow-roasting in the oven. Steaming eliminates the need to remove hot fat from the oven during roasting. Also, it renders a maximum of fat cleanly (without any roasted or caramelized bits), leaving you with lots of pure white goose fat to cook with (for ideas, see Test Kitchen, p. 134). After pouring off the fat, the goose roasts slowly for 2 to 2½ hours, making it tender and succulent, with crisp, handsomely browned skin.

regionally inspired roast turkey

Incorporate a flavored butter inspired by ingredients popular in different parts of the country, to create one of six deliciously different roast turkeys. Gravies to accompany are on p. 72. **Serves 12 to 14, with leftovers**

1   **16-lb. fresh turkey, neck, tail, and giblets reserved**
10 **Tbs. unsalted butter, softened**
    Kosher salt and freshly ground black pepper
    Regional add-ins, at right (choose 1)

Line a 12x16-inch heavy-duty roasting pan with 2 layers of paper towels. Blot the turkey dry inside and out.

In a small bowl, combine the butter with 2 tsp. salt and 1 tsp. pepper; stir in the **regional add-ins.** Set aside ¼ cup of the butter mixture for making the gravy (p. 72).

Slide your hand under the turkey's skin to loosen it from the breast and thigh meat. Using your fingers, spread the butter directly on the breast and thigh meat, being careful not to tear the skin. Season the turkey inside and out with 1½ tsp. each salt and pepper. Tuck the wings behind the neck and tie the legs together with kitchen twine.

Set the turkey breast side up in the prepared pan. Loosely cover with waxed paper or parchment and refrigerate for 1 to 2 days.

When ready to roast, uncover the turkey, discard the paper towels, and set the turkey on a V-rack in the roasting pan. Let sit for 1 hour at room temperature.

Position a rack in the lower third of the oven and heat the oven to 350°F.

Roast the turkey, basting occasionally after 1 hour and rotating the pan halfway through, until an instant-read thermometer inserted into the thickest part of the thigh registers 165°F, 2 to 2½ hours. If the skin gets too dark during roasting, tent with foil.

Tilt the turkey so the juice in the cavity runs into the roasting pan. Transfer the turkey to a platter or carving board. Remove the string, tent with foil, and let rest at room tempera-ture for at least 30 minutes and up to 1 hour before carving and serving.

Meanwhile, proceed with the gravy recipe on p. 72, at the point where the turkey has come out of the oven.

regional add-ins

NEW ENGLAND
1 Tbs. finely chopped fresh flat-leaf parsley
1 Tbs. finely chopped fresh sage
1 Tbs. finely chopped fresh thyme
½ tsp. ground cinnamon

SOUTH
2 Tbs. paprika (hot or sweet)
2 Tbs. finely chopped fresh thyme
4 tsp. minced garlic
¾ tsp. cayenne
¼ tsp. celery seed

SOUTHWEST
2 Tbs. finely chopped fresh oregano
1 Tbs. pure ancho chile powder
1 Tbs. ground cumin
½ Tbs. pure chipotle chile powder
2 tsp. minced garlic

CALIFORNIA
1 Tbs. finely chopped fresh rosemary
1 Tbs. finely chopped fresh thyme
1 Tbs. minced garlic
2 tsp. finely grated lemon zest
2 tsp. finely grated orange zest

PACIFIC NORTHWEST
¼ cup finely chopped fresh flat-leaf parsley
1 Tbs. crushed juniper berries

MIDWEST
2 Tbs. Dijon mustard
1 Tbs. finely chopped fresh sage
1 Tbs. finely chopped fresh thyme

Midwestern turkey

regionally inspired roast turkey gravy

This gravy, tailored to the recipe on p. 70, should be made ahead so it's ready when the turkey is. For best results, match the regions for your turkey and gravy flavorings! **Yields 4 cups**

Reserved neck, tail, and giblets from Regionally Inspired Roast Turkey (p. 70; do not use the liver)

1 small yellow onion, quartered

2 medium stalks celery, halved crosswise

2 Tbs. olive oil

3 cups lower-salt chicken broth

Drippings from Regionally Inspired Roast Turkey (p. 70)

Regional add-ins, at right

½ cup unbleached all-purpose flour

Kosher salt and freshly ground black pepper

Position a rack in the center of the oven and heat the oven to 400°F.

On a large rimmed baking sheet, toss the neck, tail, giblets, onion, and celery with the oil; arrange in a single layer. Roast, stirring once, until well browned, about 40 minutes.

Transfer the roasted ingredients to a heavy-duty 5-quart pot. Pour 1 cup chicken broth onto the hot baking sheet; scrape up any browned bits with a wooden spatula; transfer to the pot. Add the remaining broth and 1 quart water. Bring to a boil; lower the heat and simmer gently until reduced to 3 cups, about 1½ hours. Strain through a medium-mesh sieve into a 2-quart measuring cup; discard the solids. (The broth can be made 2 days ahead, cooled, and refrigerated. Reheat before using.)

After removing the roast turkey from the roasting pan (p. 70), pour the drippings into a fat separator and allow the fat to rise to the top. Transfer ¼ cup of the fat to a 3- to 4-quart saucepan; discard the remaining fat and add the defatted drippings to the reserved broth in the measuring cup.

Add the deglazing liquid (see right) to the roasting pan and boil over medium-high heat, scraping up any browned bits from the bottom of the pan, until reduced to ½ cup, about 10 minutes. Strain through a medium-mesh sieve set over the measuring cup of broth.

Add the reserved butter to the fat in the saucepan and melt over medium-high heat. Add the flour and cook, whisking constantly,

until slightly thickened, 3 to 4 minutes. Slowly whisk in the broth mixture; bring to a boil, then turn the heat down and simmer vigorously, whisking until the gravy is reduced to 4 cups (5 cups for the Pacific Northwest gravy), 8 to 16 minutes. Stir in **finishes** (see below) and season to taste with salt and pepper.

regional add-ins

NEW ENGLAND
Deglazing liquid: 1½ cups apple cider
Reserved butter: ¼ cup New England butter (p. 70)
Finish: 1 tsp. apple-cider vinegar

SOUTH
Deglazing liquid: 2 cups dry white wine
Reserved butter: ¼ cup Southern butter (p. 70) plus 2 bay leaves
Finishes: 2 Tbs. chopped fresh flat-leaf parsley and 2 tsp. chopped fresh thyme; discard the bay leaves

SOUTHWEST
Deglazing liquid: 2 cups dry white wine
Reserved butter: ¼ cup Southwest butter (p. 70)
Finish: 2 Tbs. honey

CALIFORNIA
Deglazing liquid: 2 cups Madeira
Reserved butter: ¼ cup California butter (p. 70)
Finish: ¼ cup fresh lemon juice

PACIFIC NORTHWEST (shown opposite)
Deglazing liquid: 2 cups dry white wine
Reserved butter: ¼ cup Pacific Northwest butter (p. 70). Add and cook 1 lb. finely chopped trimmed maitake or oyster mushrooms (4 to 5 cups), stirring often, until browned and tender, about 8 minutes. Add the flour and continue as directed.

MIDWEST
Deglazing liquid: 2 cups beer, like Budweiser®
Reserved butter: ¼ cup Midwest butter (p. 70)
Finishes: ½ cup heavy cream and 4 tsp. Dijon mustard

Pesto-Crusted Racks
of Lamb, p. 78

Beef & Lamb

Here are classic Sunday and exciting holiday roasts, plus a handful of great options for weeknights.

the recipes

sear-roasted sirloin tip steaks with café de paris butter

Based on a butter sauce created at the Café de Paris in Geneva during the 1940s, the flavored butter in this recipe is chock full of capers, mustard, shallot, and fresh herbs.

Serves 4

- ½ cup unsalted butter, softened
- 1 Tbs. tomato paste
- 2 tsp. Dijon mustard
- 1 tsp. fresh lemon juice
- ½ tsp. Worcestershire sauce
- ½ tsp. hot smoked paprika
- ¼ tsp. curry powder
  Kosher salt and freshly ground black pepper
- 1 medium shallot, minced (about ¼ cup)

- ¼ cup thinly sliced fresh chives
- 2 Tbs. chopped nonpareil capers
- 1 tsp. chopped fresh thyme
- 1½ lb. sirloin tip steaks (about 1 inch thick), cut into 4 portions
- 2 Tbs. extra-virgin olive oil

In a small bowl, mix the butter, tomato paste, mustard, lemon juice, Worcestershire, paprika, curry powder, ½ tsp. salt, and ¾ tsp. black pepper with a fork until smooth. Stir in the shallot, chives, capers, and thyme.

Transfer the butter to a large piece of plastic wrap. Using the plastic, roll the butter into a log about 2 inches in diameter; twist the ends to close. Refrigerate for at least 2 hours. (The butter can be made up to 1 week ahead.)

Position a rack in the center of the oven and heat the oven to 400°F. Season the steaks on all sides with 1 tsp. salt and ½ tsp. pepper. Heat the oil in a heavy-duty 12-inch skillet over medium-high heat until shimmering hot. Add the steaks and cook, undisturbed, until browned around the edges, 2 to 3 minutes. Flip and cook until the other side is browned, 2 minutes. Transfer the skillet to the oven.

Roast until cooked to your liking, 4 to 6 minutes for medium rare (130°F to 135°F). Transfer to a cutting board, tent with foil, and let rest for 5 minutes. Serve each steak with a slice or two of the butter on top.

roasted lamb loins with mustard-herb crust

The crunchy, sweet-and-savory breadcrumb crust is a delicious contrast to the tender, rosy-red meat of these small roasts. Serve with roasted potatoes and asparagus, if you like. **Serves 4 to 6**

- 3 Tbs. extra-virgin olive oil
- 2 medium cloves garlic, chopped
- 2 tsp. chopped fresh rosemary
- ½ cup chopped scallions (white and light-green parts only; from about 8 scallions)
  Kosher salt and freshly ground black pepper
- 1 Tbs. chopped fresh mint
- 1 Tbs. chopped fresh flat-leaf parsley
- 2 boneless single lamb loin roasts (12 to 14 oz. each), trimmed
- ½ cup panko
- 1 Tbs. Dijon mustard
- 2 tsp. honey

Position a rack in the center of the oven and heat the oven to 375°F. Arrange a flat roasting rack over a heavy-duty rimmed baking sheet.

Heat 2 Tbs. of the oil in a 10-inch skillet over medium-high heat. Add the garlic and rosemary and cook, stirring, until fragrant but not browned, about 20 seconds. Add the scallions, season with salt and pepper, and cook, stirring occasionally, until softened, 1 to 2 minutes. Add the mint and parsley and cook, stirring, for another few seconds. Remove from the heat and transfer to a medium bowl.

Pat the lamb loins dry and season with salt and pepper. Heat the remaining 1 Tbs. oil in a 12-inch skillet over medium-high heat until shimmering hot. Cook the lamb, turning once, until two sides are nicely browned, about 2 minutes per side. (Since the loins are so small, sear only the top

and bottom; you don't need to bother with the sides.) Transfer the lamb loins to the roasting rack on the baking sheet and let them cool for a couple of minutes.

Stir the panko, mustard, and honey into the scallion mixture and season to taste with salt and pepper. Divide the panko coating between the two loins, gently pressing it on so that it covers the top and comes partway down the sides. Roast the lamb until an instant-read thermometer inserted in the thickest part of a loin registers 125°F to 130°F for medium rare, 15 to 20 minutes, or 130°F to 135°F for medium, 20 to 25 minutes. Transfer the lamb to a cutting board and let it rest for 10 minutes. Slice the lamb ½ inch thick and serve; make sure to scoop up any crust that falls off the lamb and scatter it over each serving.

When arranging the lamb racks in the roasting pan, let the bones rest on the edge of the pan so the racks aren't too tightly packed together.

pesto-crusted racks of lamb

The four-step method for roasting these lamb racks—a quick sear for color and flavor, a brief rest so the meat can relax, a coating of bright, lemony parsley pesto and cheesy breadcrumbs, and then a roast in a hot oven—yields lamb that's tender, tasty, juicy, and beautiful, to boot. **Serves 8**

FOR THE CRUMB COATING

- **2** cups 1-inch-cubed fresh baguette (with crust)
- **1½** oz. (¼ cup) pine nuts, toasted
- **1** oz. finely grated Parmigiano-Reggiano (1 cup using a rasp grater)
- **1** Tbs. finely grated lemon zest (from 1 large lemon)
- **1** medium clove garlic, chopped
  Kosher salt and freshly ground black pepper

FOR THE PESTO

- **1** cup packed fresh flat-leaf parsley sprigs
- **¼** cup fresh rosemary leaves
- **6** Tbs. extra-virgin olive oil

- **1** tsp. finely grated lemon zest (from ½ small lemon)
- **1** medium clove garlic, chopped
  Kosher salt

FOR THE LAMB

- **3** 8- or 9-bone frenched lamb racks (about 1¾ lb. each)
- **2** Tbs. extra-virgin olive oil
  Flaky sea salt, for finishing

MAKE THE CRUMB COATING

Pulse the bread cubes, pine nuts, Parmigiano-Reggiano, lemon zest, garlic, ½ tsp. salt, and ½ tsp. pepper in a food processor until coarse crumbs form. Transfer to a medium bowl. (You can make

the coating up to 1 day ahead. Keep refrigerated.)

MAKE THE PESTO

Pulse the parsley, rosemary, oil, lemon zest, garlic, and ½ tsp. salt in the food processor until a coarse paste forms. (You can make the pesto up to 1 day ahead. Keep refrigerated.)

SEAR THE LAMB

Heat a heavy-duty 12-inch skillet over medium-high heat until hot. Rub the lamb racks all over with the oil and then, working with one rack at a time, sear them, meat side down, until browned, about 4 minutes each. Pour off any accumulated fat, as necessary. Let rest on a cutting board for about 20 minutes to cool. **Meanwhile, position a rack** in the center of the oven and heat the oven to 375°F.

ROAST THE RACKS

Rub one-third of the pesto over the meat side of each rack. Firmly press the crumb coating over the pesto. Arrange the racks bone side down in a large roasting pan (if the racks seem crowded, rest the bones on the edge of the pan). Roast until the crumbs are browned and a probe or instant-read thermometer inserted into the eye of the meat registers 135°F for medium rare, 25 to 30 minutes, or 145°F for medium, about 40 minutes.

Let the racks rest in the pan at room temperature for 10 to 15 minutes. Transfer to a carving board and carefully slice between the bones to make individual chops. Lightly sprinkle the cut sides of each chop with sea salt and serve with any crumb coating that fell off during carving.

shopping for racks of lamb

You'll need to buy three racks of lamb to serve 8. When shopping for them, keep the following in mind:

Look for American lamb racks for this recipe, as opposed to Australian or New Zealand lamb. American lambs are typically bigger and their meaty racks are ideal for this recipe. If you prefer or can only find Australian or New Zealand lamb racks, they'll weigh less, so to serve 8 people, buy 4 racks and expect the cooking time to be shorter.

Ask for whole lamb racks, bones 1 through 8, with the chine bones removed and the rib bones frenched. If the racks are on the smaller side (less than 1¾ lb. each), ask for an additional bone (bone 9) as well.

hanger steak with spicy miso glaze

Known for its intensely beefy flavor, hanger steak is also sometimes called "butcher's steak" because butchers often keep it for themselves. If you can't find it, you can use sirloin tip steak, but it will cook more quickly. Serve with stir-fried bok choy and jasmine rice. **Serves 4**

½ cup mirin
2 Tbs. minced shallots
2 Tbs. minced fresh ginger
1 tsp. minced garlic
1 Tbs. plus 2 tsp. grapeseed oil
2 tsp. light miso
¼ tsp. Asian hot sauce, such as Sriracha
1 1¾- to 2-lb. hanger steak, trimmed
  Kosher salt and freshly ground black pepper
¼ cup thinly sliced scallions

Position a rack in the center of the oven and heat the oven to 400°F.

Simmer the mirin, shallots, ginger, and garlic in an 8-inch skillet over medium heat until the mixture is syrupy and large bubbles start to form, about 5 minutes. Remove from the heat and whisk in 1 Tbs. of the grapeseed oil, the miso, and the hot sauce. Set aside.

Season the steaks generously with salt and pepper. Heat a 12-inch oven-safe skillet over high heat until very hot. Add the remaining 2 tsp. oil, swirling it until the pan is well coated. Cook the steaks, flipping once, until browned, about 4 minutes total.

Using a pastry brush, spread the glaze evenly over the steaks, transfer to the oven, and roast until an instant-read thermometer inserted into the thickest part of the steak reads 130°F to 135°F for medium rare, about 4 minutes.

Transfer the steaks to a cutting board, let rest for 5 minutes, and then cut on the diagonal into ½-inch-thick slices. Pour any juice remaining in the pan over top and sprinkle with the scallions.

vietnamese-style lamb riblets with sweet soy dipping sauce

Lamb riblets (which are smaller than pork spareribs) make for deliciously unexpected finger food. They're perfect party fare because you can roast them ahead of time and then run them under the broiler at the last minute to get even more caramelized flavor and crisp edges. **Serves 4 to 6**

FOR THE MARINADE

- ¼ cup finely chopped shallot
- 2 medium cloves garlic, minced
- 2 Tbs. fish sauce
- 2 Tbs. soy sauce
- 2 Tbs. peanut or vegetable oil
- 2 Tbs. packed brown sugar (light or dark)
- 1½ Tbs. fresh lime juice
- 1 Tbs. grated fresh ginger
- 1 Tbs. whole coriander seed, toasted and coarsely ground
- 1 tsp. chile sauce, such as sambal oelek or Sriracha
- ¼ tsp. kosher salt
- 2 lb. lamb breast riblets (also called Denver-style ribs)

FOR THE DIPPING SAUCE

- 2 Tbs. fish sauce
- 2 Tbs. fresh lime juice
- 2 Tbs. unseasoned rice vinegar
- 2 Tbs. chopped fresh cilantro
- 1 Tbs. soy sauce
- 1 Tbs. granulated sugar
- 1 medium clove garlic, minced

MARINATE THE RIBLETS

Put all of the marinade ingredients in a medium bowl and stir to combine. Put the riblets in a gallon-size freezer bag and pour in the marinade. Seal the bag and massage the riblets to evenly distribute the marinade. Refrigerate for at least 8 and up to 24 hours, turning the bag occasionally to redistribute the marinade.

COOK THE RIBLETS

Position a rack in the center of the oven and heat the oven to 300°F. Remove the riblets from the marinade, scraping any excess seasonings back into the bag (reserve the marinade). Arrange the riblets bone side down on a flat roasting rack in a roasting pan or on a heavy-duty baking sheet. Roast, basting with the reserved marinade every 20 minutes for the first hour, until the meat is very tender and can be easily pierced with a knife, 1½ to 2 hours. (The riblets can be roasted, cooled, and refrigerated up to 2 days ahead.)

MAKE THE DIPPING SAUCE

Combine all of the sauce ingredients in a small bowl and stir until the sugar is dissolved.

FINISH AND SERVE

Position an oven rack 5 to 6 inches from the broiling element and heat the broiler on high. Arrange the riblets cut side up on a foil-lined baking sheet and broil until browned and sizzling on one side, 2 to 3 minutes. Turn with tongs and brown the other side, 2 to 3 minutes more. Transfer to a serving platter. Serve with the dipping sauce and plenty of napkins.

spice-rubbed roast beef tenderloin with red-wine sauce

For a crowd, it's best to buy two partial tenderloins instead of one whole one. At the meat counter, request two butt tenderloins from the thicker hip portion of the tenderloin. This way, there are no thinner tail ends, and the roasts cook evenly. This beef tenderloin looks glamorous and tastes amazing, yet it's practically foolproof. The meat gets deeply browned right in the oven, which eliminates pre-searing. **Serves 8 to 10, with leftovers**

FOR THE BEEF

- 2 Tbs. extra-virgin olive oil
- 2 Tbs. finely chopped fresh thyme
- 1 Tbs. ground fennel seed
- ½ tsp. caraway seeds, coarsely ground
  Kosher salt and freshly cracked black pepper
- 2 2½-lb. beef butt tenderloins, trimmed

FOR THE SAUCE

- 2 Tbs. unsalted butter
- 1 Tbs. pure olive oil or expeller-pressed canola oil
- 4 oz. cremini mushrooms, thinly sliced (1¾ cup)
- ¼ cup thinly sliced shallot (1 medium)
- ¼ tsp. granulated sugar
  Kosher salt
- 3 large sprigs fresh thyme
- 1 tsp. cracked black peppercorns
- 1 750-ml bottle dry, hearty red wine, such as Shiraz or Zinfandel
- 2 cups lower-salt beef broth
- 1 Tbs. all-purpose flour
  Freshly ground black pepper

SEASON THE BEEF

In a small bowl, combine the olive oil, thyme, fennel, caraway, 1 Tbs. salt, and 1½ tsp. pepper. Pat the tenderloins dry with paper towels and coat them with the spice mixture, using your hands to spread it evenly; it will sparsely cover the meat.

ROAST THE BEEF

Remove the beef from the refrigerator and let sit at room temperature for about an hour before roasting. Meanwhile, position a rack in the center of the oven and heat the oven to 375°F.

Arrange the roasts on a flat rack on a large rimmed baking sheet. Roast until an instant-read thermometer inserted in the center reads 120°F for rare , 125°F to 130°F for medium rare, or 135°F for medium, 40 to 50 minutes.

MAKE THE SAUCE

Melt 1 Tbs. of the butter and the oil in a 10-inch skillet over medium heat. Add the mushrooms, shallot, sugar, and ¼ tsp. salt. Cook, stirring often, until soft and beginning to brown, about 6 minutes. Add the thyme, peppercorns, and half of the wine. Simmer briskly until the wine reduces and just covers the solids, 10 to 15 minutes.

Add the remaining wine and reduce again until the wine just covers the solids, 10 to 12 minutes more. Add the beef broth and simmer until reduced by half, about 15 minutes. Strain through a fine sieve set over a 1-quart measuring cup, pressing lightly on the solids. If you have more than 1½ cups liquid, return the sauce to the pan and simmer until reduced to 1½ cups.

Melt the remaining 1 Tbs. butter in a 1-quart saucepan over low heat. Whisk in the flour and cook, whisking often, until smooth and light beige in color, about 1 minute. Slowly add the wine reduction, whisking constantly. Bring to a simmer and cook, whisking often, until slightly thickened, about 3 minutes. Season to taste with salt and pepper.

SERVE

Let the beef rest for 15 minutes before carving crosswise into thick slices. Slice only as much as you plan to serve right away (leftovers keep better unsliced). If needed, warm the sauce over medium-low heat, whisking a few times, until barely simmering. Spoon the sauce over each serving or pass at the table.

dinner becomes brunch

Leftover roast beef tenderloin is a secret weapon for an easy, tasty brunch the next day. The meal can be as simple as roast beef sandwiches on soft rolls with horseradish mayonnaise and a few sprigs of watercress. Or for something more substantial, platter the sliced tenderloin and make it the centerpiece of a lavish buffet. Some delicious dishes to round out the meal are a crab and avocado salad, a citrusy salad of fresh grapefruit and arugula with a honey-lime vinaigrette, and biscuits or a coffee cake.

slow-roasted leg of lamb with mint and lemon

The lamb is rubbed with mint, lemon, and garlic and then roasted until juicy and tender. New potatoes and fresh peas with butter and more mint complete a perfect spring dinner. **Serves 4 with leftovers (8 without)**

- 1 **bone-in leg of lamb, 6 to 9 lb.; (see "buying leg of lamb" at right)**
- 1 **cup coarsely chopped fresh mint, plus ½ cup small fresh mint leaves**
- ¼ **cup extra-virgin olive oil**
- 3 **cloves garlic, minced**
- 2 **Tbs. fresh lemon juice**
- 2 **tsp. finely grated lemon zest (from 1 lemon)**
  Kosher salt and freshly ground black pepper
- 1 **cup dry white wine**
- 1½ **cups lower-salt chicken broth**

Put the lamb in a 4-quart, 15x10-inch glass baking dish. In a small bowl, mix the chopped mint, olive oil, garlic, lemon juice, lemon zest, 2 tsp. salt, and a few grinds of pepper. Spread the mixture over the lamb and turn to coat. Cover with plastic and refrigerate for 8 hours or overnight, turning once.

Remove the lamb from the refrigerator 1 hour before cooking. Put it on a V-rack in a 13x16-inch flameproof roasting pan. Cover the shank bone with foil. Add the reserved pelvic bone and 1 cup of water to the pan.

Position a rack in the lower third of the oven and heat the oven to 450°F.

Put the lamb in the oven and lower the heat to 350°F. Roast until an instant-read thermometer inserted in the thickest part of the leg, away from the bone, reads 135°F to 140°F for medium rare, 1½ to 2 hours.

Transfer the lamb to a warm platter and cover with aluminum foil. Let rest for at least 15 minutes.

Meanwhile, skim the fat from the top of the pan juices and then set the roasting pan over two burners on medium heat. Add the wine, and with a wooden spoon, scrape up all the browned bits. Bring to a boil and cook until the liquid has reduced to about ¼ cup. Add the broth, return to a boil, and reduce the liquid again to about 1 cup. Season to taste with salt and pepper, strain into a sauceboat, and stir in the mint leaves. Carve the lamb and serve with the sauce.

Leftover lamb will keep in the refrigerator for up to 4 days and in the freezer for up to 3 months.

buying leg of lamb

If you can, choose young lamb, which is tender, with a mild flavor. Look for firm, finely grained, pale- to dark-pink meat. The layer of fat should be smooth and white, and any cut bone should be porous, moist, and red.

A whole (or long) leg of lamb has the sirloin attached and weighs from 6 to 9 lb. It yields a range of meat, from tender and marbled to firmer and leaner. Ask your butcher not to break the shank bone but to simply cut the tendons that hold the meat to the bone; this will allow the meat to shrink from the bone while roasting. Also, ask him to give you the pelvic bone (it will lend great flavor to the sauce) and to tie the meat to form a compact shape. This will make roasting and carving easier.

beef tenderloin with roquefort-pecan butter

These tender steaks, topped with a tangy blue cheese and toasted nut butter, make for a main course that's ready in minutes but feels like you've fussed. **Serves 4**

- ½ cup pecan halves, chopped
- 4 1½-inch-thick center-cut beef tenderloin steaks (6 to 7 oz. each)
  Kosher salt and freshly ground black pepper
- 1 Tbs. vegetable oil
- 3 oz. Roquefort, at room temperature
- ¼ cup unsalted butter, softened
- 2 Tbs. whole flat-leaf parsley leaves

Position a rack in the center of the oven and heat the oven to 350°F.

Put the pecans on a small rimmed baking sheet and toast until fragrant and pale golden on the cut sides, 6 to 8 minutes. Let cool completely.

Pat the steaks dry and season with 1 tsp. salt and ½ tsp. pepper. Heat a 10-inch ovenproof, heavy-duty skillet (preferably cast iron; don't use a nonstick skillet) over medium-high heat for 2 minutes. Add the oil and swirl the skillet to coat. Add the steaks and cook, flipping once with tongs, until well browned on both sides, 6 to 7 minutes total. Transfer the skillet to the oven and cook the steaks until an instant-read thermometer registers 125°F for medium rare, 5 to 6 minutes.

Meanwhile, in a small bowl, mash together the cheese and butter with a fork and then stir in the pecans.

Remove the skillet from the oven and top the steaks with the Roquefort butter. Let the steaks rest in the pan, loosely covered with foil, for 5 minutes. Serve sprinkled with the parsley leaves.

rosemary-garlic roast leg of lamb with red potatoes

An overnight rest allows the Provençal blend of herbs and garlic that dot this leg of lamb to infuse the meat. Arranging the potatoes cut side down in a single layer beneath the lamb guarantees maximum caramelization.

Serves 6 to 8

- 1 4½-lb. bone-in shank half of a leg of lamb
- 2 to 3 large cloves garlic, sliced into ⅛-inch slivers
- 2 6-inch rosemary sprigs, separated into clusters of 3 to 5 leaves each
- 1 Tbs. freshly cracked black pepper
- 1½ Tbs. dried lavender, crushed
- 2 lb. medium red potatoes (about 10), quartered
- 3 Tbs. olive oil

  Kosher salt and freshly ground black pepper

Pat the lamb dry with paper towels. With a small paring knife, make a deep slit through the fat layer on the roast and insert a sliver of garlic and a rosemary leaf cluster. Repeat every 2 inches over the fat layer, using all of the garlic and rosemary. Sprinkle the roast with the cracked pepper and lavender.

Cover and refrigerate overnight.

Remove the meat from the refrigerator and let sit at room temperature for 30 minutes before roasting. Meanwhile, position a rack in the center of the oven and heat the oven to 375°F.

Toss the potatoes with the olive oil in a 10x15-inch (or similar) roasting pan until well coated. Season with salt and pepper and arrange cut side down in a single layer.

Sprinkle the lamb all over with 1 Tbs. salt and set it on the potatoes. Roast until an instant-read thermometer inserted in the thickest part reaches 135°F for medium rare and the potatoes are tender when pierced with a fork, about 1½ hours.

Transfer the roast to a serving platter or carving board, cover loosely with foil, and let rest for 20 to 30 minutes. Keep the potatoes warm in the turned-off oven.

Serve the roast whole or carved with the potatoes arranged around it.

how to carve a leg of lamb

For the most tender slices of lamb, you'll want to cut the meat across the grain, and that means slicing it perpendicular to the bone. To do this, grab a sharp slicing knife and follow these steps:

1 Cut off a few slices of meat parallel to the bone on the underside of the leg so it has a flat surface to rest on (not pictured). Lay the leg on the cut side and make a series of vertical slices, to your preferred thickness, down to the bone.

2 Turn the knife so that it's parallel to the bone and release the slices by making one long horizontal cut along the bone. Repeat on the remaining sides as necessary to carve all the meat from the bone.

Slow-roasting results in a beautifully rosy-pink interior, but the exterior of the roast will still be pale. After a rest period, blast the roast in a 500°F oven to brown the exterior.

slow-roasted beef standing rib roast with brown ale butter sauce

The trick to evenly cooking a large bone-in beef roast like this is to roast it at a very low temperature for a long time. This way, the meat stays evenly pink throughout. Let the meat rest (for at least an hour), then just before you're ready to serve, crank up the oven and brown it. **Serves 8 to 10**

- 1 **Tbs. fennel seeds**
- 2 **tsp. coriander seeds**
- 2 **tsp. cumin seeds**
- 1 **tsp. celery seeds**
- 1 **tsp. caraway seeds**
   Kosher salt and coarsely ground black pepper
- 1 **4-bone (9- to 10-lb.) beef standing rib roast, lightly trimmed of exterior fat and top ½ inch frenched, if desired**
- 2¼ **cups (18 oz.) brown ale, such as Newcastle®**
- 2¼ **cups lower-salt beef broth**
- 3 **Tbs. Dijon mustard**
- 4 **Tbs. cold unsalted butter, cut into 4 pieces**
   Flaky sea salt, for finishing

Mix the fennel, coriander, cumin, celery, and caraway seeds, 2 tsp. salt, and 1 tsp. pepper on a large cutting board; roll over them with a heavy rolling pin until lightly cracked. Roll the roast in the seeds to coat on all sides. Gather any remaining seeds and pat them onto the beef. Set the beef aside at room temperature for 1 hour.

Meanwhile, position a rack in the center of the oven and heat the oven to 200°F.

Position the beef bone side down in a large, heavy-duty, flame-proof roasting pan. Roast until a probe or instant-read thermometer inserted into the center of the eye registers 120°F to 125°F for rare, 130°F to 135°F for medium rare, or 145°F for medium, between 4 and 5 hours. Begin checking the temperature after 4 hours to avoid overcooking. Let the beef rest in the roasting pan, uncovered, at room temperature for 1 to 1½ hours.

Raise the oven temperature to 500°F. Return the beef to the oven and roast until the seeds begin to brown, about 12 minutes.

The easiest way to carve this roast is to first cut the meat in one piece from the bones. To do this, slice between the meat and bones, following the inner curve of the bones. Then slice the boneless roast into individual portions. You can also cut between the bones and offer them at the table, if you like.

Transfer the beef to a carving board. Pour off any fat from the roasting pan (reserve, if desired, to make Yorkshire Pudding; see Test Kitchen, p. 135). Set the roasting pan over medium-high heat, add the beer, and bring to a boil, stirring down the foam and scraping up any browned bits from the pan with a wooden spatula. Boil until the liquid is reduced to ¾ cup, 10 to 15 minutes. Whisk in the broth and mustard and continue boiling, whisking often, until reduced to about 1½ cups, about 10 minutes. Whisk in the butter just until emulsified, remove from the heat, and season to taste with salt and pepper; transfer to a gravy boat for serving.

To carve, remove the meat from the bones by running a long, thin carving knife between the eye of meat and the bones, along the interior curve of the bones. Then cut the beef into thick slices and lightly sprinkle with sea salt. Serve the beef with the sauce.

shopping for a standing rib roast

A beef rack roast is often called a standing rib roast or a prime rib roast, especially when the meat is prime grade. When shopping for one, keep the following in mind:

- Ask for a partial rack, preferably bones 1 through 4, which is known as the "first cut." This cut has a more well-defined eye of meat, so there won't be as many fatty areas, and it will easily feed 8 people.
- In some supermarkets, the roast you want—a beef standing rib roast with the ribs intact but the chine bone removed—is called a "semi-boneless rib roast."

- Never let the butcher cut the meat off the rib bones and tie it back on. This makes the roast easier to carve, but you'll lose the flavor and insulation from the bones. And beware: If you find a beef rib roast tied with butcher's twine at the supermarket, it's pretty safe to assume that the meat has been cut off the bones. If that's all they have in the case, ask the butcher to cut you a roast that's still on the bone.

Fresh Ham with Rosemary,
Garlic, and Lemon, p. 92

Pork

Play off pork's natural sweet and savory qualities with great herb combinations, bright salsas, rich pan sauces, and more.

the recipes

fresh ham with rosemary, garlic, and lemon

With just a few seasonings rubbed on a day ahead, a slow-roasted fresh ham becomes a juicy, fork-tender, and fragrant holiday centerpiece. Serve with roasted sweet potatoes and lightly sautéed green beans, if you like. **Serves 6, with leftovers**

FOR THE HAM

8½   lb. bone-in fresh half- ham, preferably shank end, rind (skin) removed
1   medium lemon
¼   cup olive oil
¼   cup fresh rosemary leaves
6   medium cloves garlic, halved
    Kosher salt and freshly ground black pepper
¼   cup white-wine vinegar

FOR THE PAN SAUCE

¼   cup dry white wine
½   cup lower-salt chicken broth
2   tsp. unsalted butter, softened
2   tsp. unbleached all-purpose flour
1   Tbs. cherry jam

PREPARE THE HAM

Set the ham fat side up in a large heavy-duty roasting pan. Use a sharp knife to score the fat in a 1-inch diamond pattern, cutting only about three-quarters of the way through the fat.

Peel the zest from the lemon with a vegetable peeler, avoiding the white pith. Put the zest, olive oil, rosemary, garlic, 1 Tbs. salt, and 1 tsp. pepper in a food processor and pulse to a coarse paste. Rub this mixture all over the ham. Cover the pan tightly with foil and refrigerate for 12 to 24 hours.

Position a rack in the oven so that the ham will sit as high as possible but still have at least 2 inches head space for air circulation. Heat the oven to 350°F.

Keep the ham covered with the foil and roast for 3 hours.

Uncover the pan and drizzle the vinegar over the ham, taking care not to wash off the coating. Continue roasting, basting every 15 minutes or so, until the ham is well browned and an instant-read thermometer inserted in the center of the meat without touching bone registers 170°F (check in several places), 1 to 1½ hours more. If the ham or drippings begin to brown too much, cover loosely with foil to prevent burning. Transfer the ham to a carving board to rest while you make the sauce.

MAKE THE SAUCE

Pour the pan drippings into a bowl, let sit until the fat rises to the top, and then skim off the fat. Return the skimmed drippings to the roasting pan and set the pan over medium heat. Whisk in the wine, scraping up any particles stuck to the pan's bottom. Whisk in the broth, add ½ cup water, and continue to boil until the liquid is reduced by one-third, about 2 minutes. Meanwhile, use a fork to mash the butter with the flour in a small bowl or ramekin to create a thick paste. Whisk the cherry jam into the sauce, then add the butter paste in parts, whisking until the paste is fully dissolved and the sauce is simmering and thickened.

Carve the ham (see Test Kitchen, p. 128) and serve with the sauce. Leftover ham will keep in the refrigerator for up to 3 days and in the freezer for up to 2 months.

pernil-style pork tenderloin

Pernil is a brightly flavored roast pork dish from the Caribbean. This version uses quick-cooking tenderloin in place of the more traditional pork shoulder, but it has the same robust flavorings, including garlic, cumin, oregano, vinegar, and lime. **Serves 4**

3	large cloves garlic, coarsely chopped
2	small shallots, coarsely chopped
4	Tbs. extra-virgin olive oil
1	Tbs. distilled white vinegar
1	tsp. chili powder
¾	tsp. ground cumin
¾	tsp. dried oregano
½	tsp. granulated sugar
	Kosher salt and freshly ground black pepper
1	1¼-lb. pork tenderloin
4	lime wedges

Position a rack in the center of the oven and heat the oven to 400°F.

In a food processor, combine the garlic, shallots, 3 Tbs. of the oil, the vinegar, chili powder, cumin, oregano, sugar, ¾ tsp. salt, and ¼ tsp. pepper. Pulse for several seconds to make a paste.

Cut the tenderloin in half crosswise and then butterfly both halves by holding a knife parallel to the cutting board and cutting a lengthwise slit to within ½ inch of the other side of the tenderloin. Spread 1 Tbs. of the paste inside each slit. Tie with kitchen string or secure with toothpicks and season with salt and pepper.

Heat a heavy-duty, ovenproof, 10-inch skillet over high heat until hot and add the remaining 1 Tbs. oil, swirling the pan to coat the bottom. Add the tenderloins and sear on all sides until golden-brown, 3 to 4 minutes total. Transfer the skillet to the oven and roast for 8 minutes. Turn the tenderloins over and spread the remaining paste on top. Roast until an instant-read thermometer inserted in the thickest part of each registers 145°F, about 6 minutes more. Transfer to a cutting board, remove the string or toothpicks, and let rest for 5 minutes. Slice ½ inch thick and serve with the lime wedges.

pork chops with cider-dijon pan sauce

An easy-to-make sauce gives everyday pork chops a flavor boost. You could make this recipe with boneless pork chops, but bone-in chops have more flavor and won't overcook as easily.
Serves 4

- 4 center-cut bone-in pork chops (2 lb.)
  Kosher salt and freshly ground black pepper
- 2 Tbs. unsalted butter
- 1 medium red apple, such as Pink Lady, Fuji, or Gala, halved, cored, and cut into small dice
- 1 medium shallot, chopped (about ⅓ cup)
- ½ tsp. chopped fresh thyme
- ½ cup apple cider
- ½ cup lower-salt chicken broth
- 1 Tbs. Dijon mustard, preferably country-style (coarse-grained)

Position a rack in the center of the oven and heat the oven to 425°F. Line a large rimmed baking sheet with aluminum foil.

Season the chops with 1 tsp. salt and ½ tsp. pepper.

Melt the butter in a 12-inch skillet over medium-high heat until the foam subsides. Working in 2 batches, cook the chops until nicely browned, about 2 minutes per side. Transfer to the baking sheet and roast until no longer pink near the bone (use a paring knife to check), about 8 minutes.

Meanwhile, lower the heat to medium and add the apple, shallot, and thyme to the skillet and cook, stirring often, until beginning to brown and soften, about 2 minutes. Add the cider, scraping any bits off the bottom of the pan, and cook until reduced by half, about 2 minutes. Add the broth and mustard and continue to cook until slightly reduced, about 2 minutes. Remove from the heat and season to taste with salt and pepper. Serve the sauce over the chops.

tuscan-style roast pork with rosemary, sage, and garlic

This juicy roast gets a flavorful, burnished crust from its time on a rotisserie grill. If you don't have a rotisserie, you can grill the pork over indirect heat for equally delicious results. Because this pork gets brined, steer clear of pork loins labeled "extra tender" or "guaranteed tender," because they've been treated with sodium phosphate and water and will be too salty. **Serves 6 to 8**

FOR THE BRINED PORK

- 3 oz. kosher salt (¾ cup if using Diamond Crystal; 6 Tbs. if using Morton)
- ¼ cup packed light brown sugar
- 3 medium cloves garlic, smashed and peeled
- 3 large sprigs fresh rosemary
- 3 large sprigs fresh sage
- 1 3-lb. all-natural boneless pork loin, trimmed of excess fat

FOR THE HERB PASTE

- 8 medium cloves garlic, peeled
- ¼ cup fresh rosemary leaves
- ¼ cup fresh sage leaves
  Kosher salt and freshly ground black pepper
- 3 Tbs. extra-virgin olive oil

BRINE THE PORK

In a 3- to 4-quart saucepan, combine the salt, sugar, garlic, and herb sprigs with 2 cups of water. Stir over high heat just until the salt and sugar dissolve. Add 6 more cups of water and cool to room temperature. Transfer to a large container, add the pork, cover, and refrigerate for 8 to 18 hours.

MAKE THE HERB PASTE

Put the garlic, rosemary, sage, 1 Tbs. salt, and 1 tsp. pepper in a large mortar and pound to a coarse paste with the pestle. Add the oil and use the pestle to work it into the garlic paste. If you don't have a mortar and pestle, combine all the ingredients in a mini food processor and pulse into a coarse paste.

BUTTERFLY AND SEASON THE PORK

Remove the pork from the brine and pat it dry (discard the brine). Butterfly the pork loin by making a horizontal slit down the length of the loin, cutting almost through to the other side. Open the meat like a book. Spread half of the herb paste over the inner surface of the roast; then fold it back to its original shape. Tie the roast at 1-inch intervals with butcher's twine and then spread the remaining herb paste over the entire outer surface.

GRILL THE PORK

Set up a grill for indirect rotisserie cooking according to the manufacturer's instructions. Heat the grill to 350°F. When ready to cook, skewer the roast lengthwise on the rotisserie spit and let it rotate on the grill, covered, until an instant-read thermometer inserted near the center of the roast registers 145°F, 35 to 45 minutes.

If you don't have a rotisserie, set up your grill for indirect grilling. Heat the grill to 350°F. Put the roast in the cool zone on the grill, and cook as directed above, turning the roast about every 10 minutes.

Remove the roast from the spit if necessary and transfer it to a cutting board. Let stand for 5 minutes, remove the string, and slice thinly. Serve hot, warm, or at room temperature.

The pork must be brined
8 to 18 hours ahead. You can
also butterfly and season
the roast with the herb paste
up to 4 hours before grilling.
Refrigerate, and then let sit
at room temperature while
you heat the grill.

pork crown roast with dried-fruit-sourdough stuffing and brandy cream sauce

Move over, turkey. This may well be the new "it" roast for the holidays, especially if you're cooking for a crowd. The center of this grand roast is filled with a hearty bread and fruit stuffing that absorbs great flavor from the pork. While the pork rests after roasting, more stuffing is baked separately so everyone at the table gets plenty. **Serves 16**

FOR THE STUFFING

- 16 cups 1-inch-cubed sourdough bread (with crust; from about 1 lb.)
- 4½ cups dry white wine (from two 750-ml bottles)
- 10 oz. dried apricots, quartered (1½ cups)
- 10 oz. dried figs, stemmed and quartered lengthwise (1½ cups)
- 7½ oz. dried tart cherries (1½ cups)
- 7½ oz. golden raisins (1½ cups)
- ½ cup unsalted butter, cut into 8 pieces
- 4 cups minced celery (from 1 bunch)
- 1 lb. shallots, minced (2½ cups)
- ¼ cup fresh thyme leaves, chopped
- ¼ cup fresh sage leaves, minced
  Kosher salt and freshly ground black pepper
- 1 cup brandy

FOR THE PORK

- 1 16-bone frenched crown roast of pork (about 12 lb.)
- ¼ cup extra-virgin olive oil
  Kosher salt and freshly ground black pepper

FOR THE SAUCE

- ⅓ cup brandy
- 2 cups lower-salt chicken broth
- 1 cup heavy cream
  Kosher salt and freshly ground black pepper
  Flaky sea salt, for finishing

MAKE THE STUFFING

Position a rack in the upper third of the oven and heat the oven to 350°F. Spread the bread cubes on a large rimmed baking sheet and bake until dry and pale golden, about 15 minutes. Let the bread cool to room temperature on the pan on a rack. (You can toast the bread up to 1 day ahead. Store at room temperature.)

Bring the wine, apricots, figs, cherries, and raisins to a boil in a 4- to 5-quart pot over medium-high heat. Lower the heat and simmer, uncovered, stirring occasionally, until the fruit is very tender and the wine is reduced to about ½ cup, about 30 minutes. Transfer the fruit mixture to an 8- to 10-quart bowl. (If the fruit is tender before the wine is reduced, transfer it with a slotted spoon to the bowl and continue to boil until the wine is reduced to ½ cup.)

Melt the butter in a 12-inch skillet over medium heat. Add the celery and shallots and cook, stirring often, until softened, about 7 minutes. Stir in the thyme, sage, 2 tsp. salt, and 2 tsp. pepper and cook, stirring, for 1 minute. Add to the fruit mixture, stir well, and let cool at room temperature for at least 1 hour and up to 6 hours.

Add the bread cubes and brandy to the fruit mixture and stir well to combine.

STUFF AND ROAST THE PORK

While making the stuffing, let the pork sit in a large heavy-duty roasting pan, with the bones pointing up, at room temperature for 30 minutes to take the chill off the meat.

Position a rack in the lower third of the oven (there should be 2 or 3 inches of headspace between the pork and the broiler element) and heat the oven to 350°F.

Rub the outside of the pork with the oil and season all over with 1 tsp. salt and 1 tsp. pepper. Spoon about half of the stuffing into the center of the roast, packing it tightly and mounding it at the top. Loosely cover the bones and the stuffing with a piece of aluminum foil. Roast for 2½ hours.

Remove the foil and continue roasting until a probe or instant-read thermometer inserted between the bones into the eye of the meat registers 150°F, 20 to 30 minutes more. Check the temperature in several places, including the interior top section of meat, to be sure the meat is up to temperature throughout. If the stuffing or bones start to get too dark at any point, return the foil to the top of the roast.

Using two large metal spatulas, transfer the whole stuffed roast to a large carving board. Reserve the juice in the pan. Let the pork rest for 30 minutes while you heat the remaining stuffing and prepare the sauce.

Increase the oven temperature to 400°F. Spoon the remaining half of the stuffing into a shallow 2-quart baking dish and bake, uncovered, until golden-brown, about 30 minutes.

shopping for a crown roast of pork

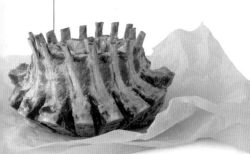

A crown roast is two pork rack roasts tied together into a round shape that looks like a crown. When shopping for one, keep the following in mind:

- Have the butcher remove the chine bones and french two complete pork rib racks, bones 1 through 8, before tying them together into the iconic crown roast. This will give you 16 ribs, which will feed 16 guests.

- If possible, examine the racks before they're tied together. The eye of meat should be well defined, and the meat should adhere closely to the bones.

MAKE THE SAUCE AND FINISH THE ROAST

Pour the reserved pan juice into a fat separator. (Or pour into a large measuring cup; let stand 5 minutes to separate, then skim off the fat.) Set the roasting pan over medium-high heat, add the brandy, and boil until reduced by half, 1 to 2 minutes. Pour the juice (leaving the fat in the separator, if using) into the roasting pan, add the broth, and bring to a boil, stirring with a wooden spatula to scrape up any browned bits from the pan. Boil until reduced to 1 cup, 5 to 8 minutes. Stir in the cream and return to a boil. Season to taste with salt and pepper; transfer to a gravy boat for serving.

To carve the roast, snip and discard the twine. Use a large chef's knife to slice between the bones. There's no need to remove the stuffing before carving. Season the meat with sea salt and serve with the stuffing and the sauce.

After removing the twine, use a large chef's knife to slice between the bones, creating large bone-in pork chops. Scoop out some of the stuffing, too, and serve the additional baked stuffing at the table.

pork tenderloin with pears and cider

A creamy sauce flavored with shallots, cider, and mustard brings together pork and fresh pears in this fabulous fall dish. Sautéed green beans and wild rice pilaf would make lovely accompaniments.

Serves 4

- 1¼ lb. pork tenderloin, trimmed
- 1 tsp. olive oil
- Kosher salt and freshly ground black pepper
- 2 Tbs. unsalted butter
- 2 firm-ripe Anjou pears, each peeled, cored, and cut into 8 wedges
- ½ cup finely chopped shallots
- 2 Tbs. sherry vinegar
- ⅔ cup pear cider or apple cider
- 3 Tbs. heavy cream
- 1½ tsp. Dijon mustard
- 2 tsp. fresh thyme, minced

Position a rack in the center of the oven and heat the oven to 500°F.

Pat the pork dry, rub it with the oil, and season generously with salt and pepper. Heat a heavy-duty 12-inch skillet over medium-high heat until very hot, and then sear the pork on all sides until golden-brown, about 6 minutes total. Transfer to a small rimmed baking sheet and roast until an instant-read thermometer inserted into the thickest part registers 140°F, 10 to 15 minutes. Transfer the pork to a cutting board, tent with foil, and let rest for 5 minutes.

Meanwhile, melt 1 Tbs. of the butter in the skillet over medium-high heat. Add the pears in a single layer and cook, flipping once, until just tender and lightly browned, about 3 minutes per side. Transfer to a plate and keep warm.

Add the remaining 1 Tbs. butter and the shallots to the skillet and cook, stirring, over medium heat until the shallots are just beginning to turn golden, 2 to 3 minutes. Add the vinegar and stir, scraping up any brown bits. Add the cider and cook until slightly reduced, 2 to 3 minutes. Whisk in the heavy cream, mustard, and thyme and cook until slightly thickened, about 3 minutes. Season to taste with salt and pepper.

Slice the pork and serve with the sauce and pears.

tuscan roast pork with yellow potatoes, fennel, and parsnips

For this slow roast, the potatoes and vegetables are precooked so they come out perfectly tender when the pork loin is done. The rosemary, coriander, fennel seeds, and other Tuscan flavors rubbed over the pork also season the juice it releases, which creates a delicious jus for serving. **Serves 6**

- ¼ cup plus 1 Tbs. extra-virgin olive oil
- 2 Tbs. sambuca
- 4 large cloves garlic, minced
- 2 Tbs. finely chopped fresh rosemary
- 2 tsp. dried fennel seeds, crushed
- 1 tsp. ground coriander
  Kosher salt and freshly ground black pepper
- 1 3-lb. boneless pork loin (have your butcher leave ⅛ inch fat on the top)
- 1½ lb. small yellow potatoes (about 10), halved
- 3 medium parsnips, peeled, cut lengthwise into quarters, and cored
- 2 medium sweet onions, halved lengthwise and cut into ¼-inch slices
- 1 large fennel bulb, stalks trimmed, bulb quartered, cored, and cut lengthwise into ¼-inch slices (fronds reserved)
- 1½ cups lower-salt chicken broth
- ¾ cup dry white wine

In a small bowl, combine 1 Tbs. each of the oil and sambuca with the garlic, rosemary, fennel seeds, coriander, 1½ Tbs. salt, and ¾ tsp. pepper to make a paste; set aside.

Pat the roast dry with paper towels. Rub the paste over the entire roast.

Cover and refrigerate overnight.

Position a rack in the center of the oven and heat the oven to 400°F.

Arrange the potatoes, parsnips, onions, and fennel in a 13x17-inch (or similar) roasting pan, season with ½ tsp. salt and ⅛ tsp. pepper, and drizzle with the remaining ¼ cup olive oil. Roast, turning occasionally, until a fork inserted in the center of each type of vegetable meets little resistance, about 40 minutes.

Meanwhile, remove the roast from the refrigerator and let sit at room temperature for 30 minutes.

Reduce the oven temperature to 300°F. Put the roast, fat side up, on top of the vegetables. Add the chicken broth and wine, and roast, basting the meat and vegetables occasionally, until an instant-read thermometer inserted into the roast registers 135°F to 140°F, about 2 hours.

Transfer the roast to a serving platter or carving board, cover loosely with foil, and let rest for 20 to 30 minutes. With a slotted spoon, transfer the vegetables to a large sheet of foil; wrap and keep warm in the turned-off oven.

Pour the juice from the roasting pan into a fat separator and let sit until the fat rises to the top. Pour the clear juice into a 1-quart saucepan, leaving the fat behind, and put over medium-high heat. Add the remaining 1 Tbs. sambuca and simmer until the jus is slightly reduced, 3 to 5 minutes. Strain through a fine sieve and season to taste with salt and pepper.

Arrange the pork on a platter with the vegetables, garnish with the fennel fronds, and serve with the jus on the side.

glazed pork loin with pineapple-scallion chutney

In this take on the classic pairing of pineapple and ham, fruit is used in a delicious maple-infused glaze and sweet-spicy chutney for roast pork. If possible, use grade B maple syrup in the glaze; it has a more robust flavor than lighter grades. **Serves 6 to 8**

2	**large cloves garlic**
	Kosher salt
1	**Tbs. extra-virgin olive oil**
2	**tsp. finely grated lemon zest**
1½	**tsp. toasted coriander seeds, ground**
1	**3-lb. boneless pork loin roast**
1	**medium fresh pineapple (about 3½ lb.)**
¼	**cup maple syrup, preferably grade B**
2	**Tbs. sherry vinegar**
1	**large shallot, minced**
	Pinch ground cayenne
1	**large scallion, thinly sliced, white and green parts separated**
3	**Tbs. chopped fresh cilantro**

Peel and coarsely chop the garlic. Sprinkle it with a generous pinch of salt and mash it to a paste with the side of a chef's knife. Transfer to a small bowl and stir in the oil, lemon zest, coriander, and 1 Tbs. salt.

Put the pork on a large rimmed baking sheet, pat dry with paper towels, and rub all over with the salt mixture. Let sit at room temperature for at least 1 hour and up to 2 hours.

Position a rack in the center of the oven and heat the oven to 350°F. Roast the pork until an instant-read thermometer inserted in the thickest part reads 130°F, about 50 minutes.

Meanwhile, trim the pineapple by slicing the top, bottom, and all rind off. Remove any remaining eyes with a paring knife. Quarter the pineapple lengthwise and trim the core from each quarter. Cut half of the pineapple into small dice and roughly chop the other half. Purée the roughly chopped pineapple in a blender, then strain it through a fine strainer, pressing on the solids with a spoon, to yield about ¾ cup juice. In a small saucepan, combine the strained pineapple juice and maple syrup and cook over medium-high heat until reduced to ⅓ cup, 12 to 15 minutes. The liquid will become very bubbly as it reduces; lower the heat as necessary.

Set aside all but 2 Tbs. of the reduced liquid (this will be your glaze). Add the vinegar, shallot, cayenne, and a pinch of salt to the 2 Tbs. liquid remaining in the saucepan and cook over medium heat just until the shallot begins to soften, about 2 minutes. Add the diced pineapple and scallion whites and continue to cook, stirring frequently, until the pineapple softens and releases some of its juice, 3 to 5 minutes. Remove from the heat and let cool slightly.

When the pork reaches 130°F, brush it with some of the glaze and continue to roast, brushing with more glaze every 5 minutes, until an instant-read thermometer inserted in the center of the roast reads 145°F, about 20 minutes more. Let rest for at least 10 minutes before serving.

When ready to serve, stir the scallion greens and cilantro into the chutney. Slice the pork into ½-inch-thick rounds and serve with the chutney.

pork chops stuffed with pine nuts and herbs

A take on traditional pesto, the filling for these pork chops is amped up with sweet raisins and fresh herbs. Roast some potatoes and broccoli to serve with the chops.

Serves 6

6	center-cut, bone-in pork loin chops (1¼ inches to 1½ inches thick)
½	cup fresh mint
½	cup fresh parsley
⅓	cup fresh tarragon
⅓	cup finely grated pecorino romano (¼ oz.)
5	Tbs. extra-virgin olive oil
3	medium cloves garlic, peeled
1	tsp. finely grated lemon zest
	Kosher salt and freshly ground black pepper
¾	cup pine nuts, toasted
⅓	cup golden raisins
1	Tbs. unsalted butter, cut into 6 pieces

Position a rack in the center of the oven and heat the oven to 400°F.

With a sharp knife, make a horizontal slit in each pork chop to create a 3½-inch-long pocket.

In a food processor, combine the mint, parsley, tarragon, pecorino, 3 Tbs. of the oil, the garlic, lemon zest, ½ tsp. salt, and ¼ tsp. pepper. Pulse until finely chopped. Add ½ cup of the pine nuts and pulse until the nuts are roughly chopped. Stir in the remaining ¼ cup pine nuts and the raisins. Season the insides of the pockets with salt and pepper and stuff with the filling. Secure the pockets with toothpicks. Season the outside of the meat generously with salt and pepper.

Heat 1 Tbs. of the oil in a 12-inch skillet over medium-high heat until shimmering hot. Sear 3 of the pork chops on both sides until well browned, about 6 minutes total; transfer to a large rimmed baking sheet. Repeat with the remaining 1 Tbs. oil and the remaining pork chops. Top each chop with a piece of butter and roast in the oven until an instant-read thermometer inserted into the thickest part of the pork chops registers 145°F, 10 to 12 minutes. Discard the toothpicks and serve drizzled with the pan juice.

slow-roasted pork shoulder with carrots, onions, and garlic

Start this recipe at least a day ahead. Serve the pork and vegetables with mashed potatoes or with beans (like cranberry or cannellini) seasoned with pounded garlic, extra-virgin olive oil, and sage. **Serves 4 with leftovers (or 8 without)**

	Kosher salt and freshly ground black pepper
1	6¾- to 7-lb. boneless pork shoulder roast
1	large yellow onion, cut into ½-inch-thick rings
3	medium carrots, cut into sticks ½ inch wide and 2 to 2½ inches long
10	cloves garlic, peeled
1	cup dry white wine

Combine 2 Tbs. salt and 2 tsp. pepper in a small bowl and rub the mixture all over the pork. Put the pork, fat side up, in a large roasting pan (about 12x16x3 inches). Cover and refrigerate overnight or for up to 3 days.

Remove the pork from the refrigerator and let sit at room temperature for 1 to 1½ hours before cooking.

Position a rack in the center of the oven and heat the oven to 300°F. Uncover the pork and roast until tender everywhere but the very center when pierced with a fork, 4 to 4½ hours. Add the onion, carrots, garlic, wine, and 1 cup water to the roasting pan and continue to roast, stirring the vegetables occasionally, until the pork is completely tender, about 1 hour more.

Remove the roast from the oven and raise the oven temperature to 375°F. Using tongs, separate the pork into 8 to 10 large, rustic chunks and spread out on the pan. If most of the liquid has evaporated, add a splash more water to the pan to create a little more juice. (It shouldn't be soupy.) Return the pork to the oven and continue to roast until nicely browned on the newly exposed surfaces, about 15 minutes. Remove the pan from the oven, transfer the meat and vegetables to a serving platter, and tent loosely with foil. Let rest for 20 minutes. Skim the excess fat from the juices and serve the juices with the vegetables and meat.

shred leftovers

After dinner, pull (or hand-shred) any leftover pork. To do this, cut the chunks of pork across the grain into about 1-inch widths and pull the pork apart into pieces. Save any leftover juices separately. Well-wrapped leftovers will keep in the refrigerator for 3 to 4 days, or in the freezer for up to 2 months. See recipes for leftovers on pp. 113 and 116.

roast pork with crisp crackling and red currant gravy

Be sure to offer everyone some of the fragrant onion-orange stuffing and crunchy crackling along with their slices of juicy pork. The gravy gets its deep sweet-and-savory flavor from homemade stock, the roast drippings, creamy Danish blue cheese, and red currant jelly. **Serves 8**

FOR THE PORK

- 2 Tbs. salted butter
- 1 medium yellow onion, halved and thinly sliced
- 3 medium cloves garlic, finely chopped
- 1 Tbs. fresh thyme
- 6½ lb. skin-on boneless pork loin roast, fat trimmed to ¼ inch (see Test Kitchen, p. 133)
  - Kosher salt and freshly ground black pepper
- 1 medium orange, halved and cut crosswise ⅛ inch thick

FOR THE GRAVY

- 2½ cups Red-Wine Chicken Stock (recipe, p. 134) or lower-salt chicken broth
- 4 Tbs. salted butter
- 1⅛ oz. (¼ cup) unbleached all-purpose flour
- ½ cup heavy cream
- 2 Tbs. red currant jelly
- 1 Tbs. crumbled Danish blue cheese
  - Kosher salt and freshly ground black pepper

ROAST THE PORK

Position a rack in the center of the oven and heat the oven to 400°F.

Melt the butter in a 10-inch skillet over medium heat. Add the onion and cook, stirring occasionally, until golden and tender, about 10 minutes. Add the garlic and thyme and cook for 1 minute more. Transfer to a plate; let cool.

Remove the piece of skin and fat from the top of the roast. Using a sharp knife, score the skin crosswise through to the fat at ½-inch intervals; set aside. Score the meat in a crosshatch pattern, cutting about ½ inch deep. Season generously with salt and pepper, and spread the onion-garlic mixture over the surface. Lay the orange slices on top, replace the skin and fat, and tie the roast with twine crosswise at 1½-inch intervals. Generously season the skin with salt. (See p. 133 for photos of prepping the roast.)

Transfer to a large rimmed baking sheet and roast until an instant-read thermometer inserted in the center of the roast reads 145°F, about 1½ hours.

Transfer the roast to a cutting board and let rest for at least 30 minutes and up to 1 hour.

MAKE THE GRAVY

Meanwhile, pour off and discard the fat from the baking sheet; set aside. In a 1-quart saucepan, bring the chicken stock to a simmer. Pour 1 cup of the stock onto the baking sheet and stir, scraping up the browned bits. Pour through a medium-mesh sieve back into the saucepan and keep warm over low heat. (At this point, if the skin is not completely crisp and bubbly, untie it from the roast, put it back on the baking sheet, and bake until it is. Lay it back on top of the roast.)

Melt the butter in a 2-quart saucepan over medium-low heat. Add the flour and stir constantly until caramel color, 3 to 5 minutes. Whisk in the stock and simmer, whisking often, until the flour taste is gone, 5 to 10 minutes. Add the cream, jelly, and blue cheese and simmer, whisking often, until the gravy is smooth and thick enough to coat the back of a spoon, about 5 minutes. Season to taste with salt and pepper.

SERVE

Remove and discard the twine (if you haven't already) and carve the pork as shown below. Include crackling and orange-onion stuffing with each portion and serve with the gravy.

Use the score marks in the crackling as entry points for carving; the crackling will be too hard to cut through otherwise, and the score marks will ensure even ½-inch-thick slices.

Moussaka Gratinée, p. 108

Leftovers

Have any ham, turkey, pork, or lamb left? Here are creative and delicious ways to use it up.

the recipes

moussaka gratinée

Traditionally, Greek moussaka is a baked dish of layered eggplant, lamb, tomatoes, and potato. This modern version doesn't use potato and is baked in individual ramekins. You can prepare the filling ahead and top with the sauce just before baking. **Serves 6**

4   small eggplant (about 5 inches long), peeled, trimmed, and cut into ½-inch pieces (about 8 cups)

    Kosher salt

¼   cup extra-virgin olive oil

1   large yellow onion, finely chopped

1   lb. leftover Slow-Roasted Leg of Lamb (see p. 84), trimmed of excess fat and sinew and cut into ½-inch dice

2   cloves garlic, finely chopped

1   Tbs. tomato paste

1½   tsp. ground cinnamon

    Sea salt

½   cup strained leftover sauce from the Slow-Roasted Leg of Lamb (see p. 84)

3   Tbs. chopped fresh flat-leaf parsley

    Freshly ground black pepper

1½   cups whole milk

1   fresh bay leaf

    Pinch ground mace

2   Tbs. unsalted butter

2   Tbs. unbleached all-purpose flour

1   large egg yolk

2   oz. kefalotyri or pecorino, finely grated (about 1½ cups)

1   large egg white

Put the eggplant in a colander set over a bowl, sprinkle generously with kosher salt, and set aside.

In a 12-inch skillet, heat 2 Tbs. of the olive oil over medium-low heat. Add the onion and cook, stirring occasionally, until softened, about 10 minutes.

Raise the heat to medium high and add the lamb, stirring until it browns lightly and begins to stick to the pan, about 6 minutes. Lower the heat and add the garlic, tomato paste, cinnamon, and 1 tsp. sea salt. Pour in the sauce and stir to deglaze the pan. Cook, stirring frequently, until the liquid is slightly reduced but the lamb is still moist, 1 to 2 min-utes. Stir in the parsley and season with pepper. Transfer to a large bowl and set aside.

Wash and dry the skillet. Pat the eggplant dry with paper towels. Heat the remaining 2 Tbs. olive oil in the pan over medium-high heat. When hot, add the eggplant and cook, stirring occasionally, until lightly browned in spots, about 2 minutes. Reduce the heat to medium low, cover, and cook until soft, about 10 minutes.

Position a rack in the center of the oven and heat the oven to 400°F.

Uncover and stir the eggplant with a wooden spoon, scraping the browned bits from the bottom of the pan. Remove from the heat and mash the eggplant with the back of the spoon. Stir the eggplant into the lamb mixture and season to taste with salt and pepper. Spoon the mixture into six 8-oz. ramekins. (French onion soup bowls would work, too.)

Put the milk in a 2-quart saucepan with the bay leaf and mace. Bring to a boil over medium heat. Remove from the heat, cover, and let sit for 10 minutes to infuse the milk. Strain into a liquid measuring cup and set aside.

In a 4-quart saucepan, melt the butter over medium heat. Add the flour, stirring constantly, and cook until the mixture is lightly colored, about 2 minutes. Whisk in the reserved milk and cook, whisking constantly, until thickened and shiny, 3 to 4 minutes. Put the egg yolk in a small bowl and whisk with about ¼ cup of the sauce. Add the yolk and sauce back to the saucepan and whisk to combine. Whisk in the cheese. Remove from the heat and let cool slightly.

In a small bowl, whisk the egg white until stiff peaks form and then fold the white into the cooled sauce. Spoon the sauce over the top of the eggplant and lamb mixture, dividing evenly.

Put the ramekins in a 4-quart, 15x10-inch glass baking dish, add 1 cup of water to the dish, cover with foil, and bake for 15 min-utes. Uncover and continue baking until bubbling and browned, about 35 minutes more. Let cool for 10 minutes and serve.

lamb niçoise salad with potatoes and fava beans

Cold roasted lamb replaces the more typical tuna in this take on the classic Niçoise salad. **Serves 4**

FOR THE DRESSING

- 1 large egg yolk
- 6 oil-packed anchovies, finely chopped
- 1 clove garlic, finely chopped
- 1 tsp. Dijon mustard
- ½ cup extra-virgin olive oil
- 1 Tbs. fresh lemon juice
  Kosher salt and freshly ground black pepper

FOR THE SALAD

- 1 cup thinly sliced red onion
- 16 baby potatoes
  Kosher salt
- 2 lb. fava beans in the pod or ½ lb. haricots verts
- 16 cherry tomatoes cut in half
- ¼ cup Niçoise olives (about 20)
  Freshly ground black pepper

- ¾ lb. leftover roast lamb, thinly sliced
- 8 large caper berries

MAKE THE DRESSING

Put the egg yolk, anchovies, garlic, and mustard in a food processor. With the motor running, gradually add the olive oil and process until the mixture starts to thicken and emulsify (it should have the consistency of heavy cream), about 2 minutes. With the motor still running, add the lemon juice and 1 tsp. hot water. Continue to process until the mixture reaches a soft mayonnaise consistency. Season to taste with salt and pepper and set aside.

MAKE THE SALAD

Put the onion in a medium bowl, cover with cold water, and soak for 20 minutes. Drain and pat dry.

Put the potatoes in a large pot of well-salted water. Bring to a boil over medium-high heat and cook until the potatoes are tender, 5 to 10 minutes. Drain and when cool enough to handle, cut them in half.

Transfer to a large bowl and toss with the reserved onion and a couple of spoonfuls of the dressing.

Bring a large pot of well-salted water to a boil over medium-high heat. Remove the fava beans from their pods and cook them in the boiling water until tender, about 2 minutes. Drain and run under cold water to stop the cooking. Pinch the dull, olive-colored skin and slip each bean out (you should have about 2 cups beans). Discard the skins. (Alternatively, cook the haricots verts in the water until tender, 2 to 3 minutes.)

In a medium bowl, toss the tomatoes with the olives and season with a few grinds of pepper.

Arrange the potatoes and onions, tomatoes and olives, favas, and lamb on a large serving platter. Garnish with the caper berries. Drizzle with the remaining dressing and season to taste with salt and pepper.

Note: This recipe contains a raw egg. If that's a concern, use a pasteurized egg.

turkey bolognese

For a spin on the classic, we've replaced the customary ground meat with diced roast turkey. There's enough of this flavorful sauce to coat one pound of your favorite pasta. Try it with a sturdy shape like rigatoni or penne. For a smoky flavor, substitute bacon for the pancetta. **Yields 5½ cups**

½   **lb. pancetta, finely diced**

¼   **cup finely chopped carrot**

¼   **cup finely chopped yellow onion**

¼   **cup finely chopped celery**

4   **medium cloves garlic, minced**

1½ **tsp. fennel seed, lightly crushed**

¼   **to ½ tsp. crushed red pepper flakes**

1   **28-oz. can diced tomatoes with juice**

1   **cup dry white wine**

1   **cup homemade turkey broth or lower-salt canned chicken broth**

1   **cup whole milk**

½   **cup packed flat-leaf parsley**

2   **dried bay leaves**
     Kosher salt

4   **cups medium-diced roast turkey**

Heat a wide, heavy-duty 6- to 8-quart pot over medium heat. Add the pancetta and cook until its fat begins to render, 2 to 3 minutes. Add the carrot, onion, celery, and garlic and cook until the vegetables begin to brown, 4 to 6 minutes. Stir in the fennel seed and pepper flakes.

Add the tomatoes and white wine. Boil for 2 to 3 minutes, then add the broth, milk, parsley, and bay leaves. Stir well, return to a boil, and season with a little salt. (You should underseason, as the sauce will reduce and concentrate the salt.) Lower the heat to medium low and simmer until reduced by about one-third, 30 to 40 minutes.

Add the turkey, raise the heat to medium, and bring to a boil. Reduce the heat to medium low and simmer until the flavors are fully developed and the sauce is thick and rich, 10 to 15 minutes. Discard the bay leaves and season to taste with salt.

turkey soup with dill, parsley, and chive dumplings

A roasted turkey carcass produces rich broth that makes for a delicious turkey soup. This version incorporates airy herb-flecked dumplings.

Serves 6

FOR THE TURKEY BROTH

- 2 medium carrots, cut into 2-inch pieces
- 2 medium celery stalks, cut into 2-inch pieces
- 1 medium yellow onion, cut into quarters
- 2 dried bay leaves
- 1 cup dry white wine
- 1 roasted turkey carcass, broken in half, plus any leftover bones

FOR THE SOUP

- 2 Tbs. extra-virgin olive oil
- ½ medium yellow onion, finely diced
- 4 medium carrots, quartered lengthwise and cut into ½-inch pieces
- 4 medium parsnips, quartered lengthwise, cored, and cut into ½-inch pieces
- 1½ cups small-diced celery root
  Kosher salt and freshly ground black pepper
- 1 14½-oz. can diced tomatoes with juice
- ½ cup dry white wine
- 1 dried bay leaf
- 3 cups medium-diced roast turkey
- 2 cups chopped Swiss chard leaves (ribs removed)

FOR THE DUMPLINGS

- 6 Tbs. unsalted butter
- 2 tsp. kosher salt
- ¾ cup unbleached all-purpose flour
- 3 large eggs
- 1 Tbs. chopped fresh dill
- 1 Tbs. chopped fresh parsley
- 1 Tbs. chopped fresh chives

MAKE THE BROTH

In a 10-quart pot, combine the carrots, celery, onion, bay leaves, wine, carcass, and bones. Add 7 quarts of water and bring to a simmer over medium-high heat. Reduce the heat and simmer gently until the broth is rich and flavorful, 4 to 6 hours. Strain the broth through a fine sieve and discard the solids. Let cool; then skim off and discard the fat on the surface. The broth may be refrigerated for up to 2 days or frozen for up to 2 months.

MAKE THE SOUP

Heat the oil in a heavy-duty 6- to 8-quart pot over medium-high heat. Add the onion and cook until starting to brown, about 2 minutes. Add the carrots, parsnips, and celery root and cook until the vegetables start to color, about 4 minutes. Season with salt and pepper.

Add the tomatoes, wine, and bay leaf and bring to a boil. Add 2 quarts of the turkey broth and return to a boil. Reduce the heat and simmer until the vegetables are tender, 10 to 15 minutes. Season to taste with salt and pepper.

Add the turkey and Swiss chard and simmer until the chard is wilted, about 5 minutes. (The soup may be cooled and refrigerated for up to 2 days. Bring to a simmer before continuing.)

MAKE THE DUMPLING BATTER

In a 3-quart saucepan, bring ¾ cup water and the butter and salt to a boil over medium heat. When the butter melts, remove the pan from the heat and stir in the flour until thoroughly combined. Return the pan to medium heat and stir until the mixture pulls away from the sides of the pan.

Scrape the dough into a large bowl. With a sturdy wooden spoon, beat in the eggs, one by one, until the batter is smooth. Fold in the chopped herbs. (The batter may be covered and refrigerated for up to 1 day.)

FINISH THE SOUP WITH THE DUMPLINGS

Using two ½-teaspoon measures, drop spoonfuls of batter into the simmering soup until all of the batter is used. After the dumplings rise to the top, cover the pan and steam the dumplings until they have puffed up to double their size, about 4 minutes. Serve hot.

ham lo mein with shiitake and snow peas

Look for fresh Chinese egg noodles at Asian markets or in the produce section of the supermarket (near the wonton wrappers and tofu).

Serves 4

- 8   dried shiitake mushrooms (⅜ oz.)
- ¾   lb. fresh Chinese egg noodles
- 3   Tbs. soy sauce
- ½   Tbs. Asian sesame oil
- 3   Tbs. peanut oil
- 4   medium scallions, trimmed and thinly sliced (½ cup)
- 3   medium cloves garlic, minced
- 2   Tbs. minced fresh ginger
- ½   lb. leftover roasted fresh ham, any seasonings removed, cut into thin strips (2 cups)
- 6   oz. snow peas, trimmed and thinly sliced lengthwise (2½ cups)
- 1   medium red bell pepper, cored, seeded, and thinly sliced (2 cups)
- 1   Tbs. oyster sauce
- 1   Tbs. Chinese chile or chile-garlic paste

Rinse the mushrooms; then soak them in a small bowl in ¾ cup boiling hot water until softened, 20 to 30 minutes.

Meanwhile, in a 4-quart saucepan, bring about 2 quarts of water to a boil over high heat. Boil the noodles until barely tender, about 2 minutes. Drain, toss with 1 Tbs. of the soy sauce and the sesame oil, and spread on a baking sheet.

When the mushrooms are soft, pluck them from the water and squeeze them dry (reserve the soaking liquid). Trim off the stems and thinly slice the caps.

Heat a wok or wok pan over medium-high heat for a couple of minutes and then swirl in the peanut oil. Add the scallions, garlic, and ginger; stir-fry for 30 seconds.

Add the ham, snow peas, bell pepper, and mushrooms. Stir-fry until the bell pepper strips begin to soften, 2 minutes.

Add the reserved soaking liquid, the remaining 2 Tbs. soy sauce, the oyster sauce, and chile paste. Cook until the sauce bubbles, about 1 minute.

Add the cooked noodles and toss until most of the sauce has been absorbed, less than a minute. Serve immediately.

pulled-pork sandwiches with cabbage, caper, and herb slaw

For these sandwiches, the bread should be very lightly toasted so that it's soft and warm but not dry. Be sure to use every last bit of the juices and drizzle every last drop of vinegar onto the sandwich. Both steps improve the flavor and moisten the bread, which is key. **Serves 4**

1½	**Tbs. capers, preferably salt-packed**
2	**cups very thinly sliced green cabbage**
¼	**small red onion, very thinly sliced**
¼	**cup chopped fresh flat-leaf parsley**
3	**Tbs. thinly sliced fresh chives**
1½	**tsp. finely chopped fresh oregano**
1–2	**tsp. finely chopped preserved red chiles, or substitute Asian chile sauce (optional)**
2	**Tbs. red-wine vinegar**
	Kosher salt
3½	**cups leftover shredded pork shoulder**
1	**baguette**
3	**Tbs. extra-virgin olive oil; more to taste**

Position a rack in the center of the oven and heat the oven to 350°F.

Rinse the capers well. If using salt-packed capers, soak them in warm water for at least 5 minutes. (They should taste capery rather than salty; if not, continue soaking for a little longer.) Drain the capers and, unless they're very small, coarsely chop them.

Combine the capers, cabbage, red onion, parsley, chives, oregano, and chiles (if using). Add the vinegar and ¼ tsp. salt, toss well, and let sit at room temperature for at least 30 minutes. Toss again and season to taste with more salt or chile.

Meanwhile, put the pork in a small baking dish. (If you have any juices left, scrape them into the dish, skimming and discarding as much of the congealed fat as possible.) Cover with foil and bake the pork until warmed through, 10 to 15 minutes. Remove the pork from the oven, position a rack 6 inches from the broiler, and heat the broiler to high.

Cut the baguette crosswise into 4 equal portions (each 5 to 6 inches long) and then slice each piece horizontally so that it opens like a book. Just before serving, put the baguette pieces on a baking sheet, opening each as much as possible, and toast very lightly under the broiler, 2 to 3 minutes. Divide the pork into 4 equal portions and mound on the bottom half of each piece of baguette. Drizzle any pan juices over the pork and then pile on the cabbage slaw. Drizzle the olive oil over the slaw. If any vinegar has collected on the bottom of the slaw bowl, distribute it among the sandwiches, and serve.

turkey noodle casserole

Turkey is combined with earthy mushrooms, a creamy cheese sauce, and a crunchy, sage-scented crumb topping to make this tasty, comforting dish. You can substitute wide egg noodles for the pappardelle. **Serves 6 to 8**

- 4 Tbs. unsalted butter; more for the baking dish
- Kosher salt
- ¾ cup coarse dry breadcrumbs
- 2 Tbs. extra-virgin olive oil
- 1 Tbs. freshly grated Parmigiano-Reggiano
- 1 Tbs. finely chopped fresh sage
- Freshly ground black pepper
- 1 lb. assorted fresh mushrooms, cleaned and sliced ⅛ to ¼ inch thick
- 3 Tbs. minced shallot
- 2 medium cloves garlic, minced
- ½ cup all-purpose flour
- 6 cups low-fat milk
- 3½ oz. (1½ cups) grated sharp white Cheddar
- 3 Tbs. finely chopped fresh flat-leaf parsley
- 8 oz. egg pappardelle pasta
- 3 cups shredded or diced roast turkey

Position a rack in the center of the oven and heat the oven to 350°F.

Butter a 3-quart baking dish. Bring a large pot of well-salted water to a boil over high heat.

Mix the breadcrumbs, 1 Tbs. of the olive oil, Parmigiano, and sage in a small bowl. Season to taste with salt and pepper. Set aside.

Heat a large (12-inch) skillet over medium heat. Add the remaining 1 Tbs. olive oil to the pan and then add the mushrooms; cook, stirring frequently, until softened and golden on the edges, about 10 minutes. Reduce the heat to medium low and add the shallot and garlic; cook, stirring until softened, about 2 minutes. Season to taste with salt and pepper and set aside.

Melt the butter in a 4-quart saucepan over medium heat. Add the flour and whisk constantly until it colors slightly, 2 to 3 minutes. Remove the pan from the heat and gradually whisk in enough of the milk to form a thick, smooth paste. Set the pan back over the heat and whisk in the remaining milk in a steady stream. Add 1 tsp. of salt. Bring to a boil over medium-high heat, whisking constantly. Reduce the heat to medium low and simmer for 3 minutes, whisking constantly. Turn off the heat and stir in the Cheddar and parsley. Season to taste with more salt and pepper. Set aside.

Cook the pasta in the boiling water until al dente, about 1 minute less than package timing. Drain and spread the pasta in an even layer on the bottom of the prepared baking dish. Sprinkle the turkey and mushrooms over the pasta. Pour the sauce on top and use a fork to distribute it evenly.

Sprinkle the breadcrumbs over the entire casserole. Set on a baking sheet to catch drips and bake until golden-brown and bubbling, 50 to 60 minutes. Let rest 20 to 30 minutes before serving.

indian lamb curry with green beans and cashews

For spicier results, leave the ribs in the chile when you remove the seeds.

Serves 4

- 2 Tbs. unsalted butter or ghee
- 2 medium red onions, sliced ¼ inch thick (about 4 cups)
- 1 1½-inch piece fresh ginger, peeled and finely chopped (about 1½ Tbs.)
- 6 green cardamom pods, smashed
- 2 cloves garlic, minced
- 2½ tsp. garam masala
- 1 serrano chile, seeded and diced
- 1 fresh bay leaf
  Kosher salt
- 2 cups lower-salt chicken broth
- 1 lb. russet potatoes (about 2 large), peeled and cut into ½-inch dice
- 12 oz. green beans, trimmed and cut into 2-inch lengths (about 4 cups)
- 1 lb. leftover roast lamb, cut into ½-inch pieces
- ½ cup toasted unsalted cashews
- 3 Tbs. chopped fresh cilantro
- ½ tsp. fresh lemon juice; more to taste

In a 12-inch skillet, melt the butter over medium heat. Add the onions and cook, stirring frequently, until softened but not browned, about 10 minutes.

Stir in the ginger, cardamom, garlic, 2 tsp. of the garam masala, the chile, bay leaf, and 1½ tsp. salt and cook until fragrant, about 1 minute. Pour in the broth and bring to a boil. Add the potatoes and lower the heat to medium low so the broth simmers gently. Cook uncovered, stirring occasionally, until the potatoes are tender, 20 to 25 minutes.

Meanwhile, bring a large pot of salted water to a boil. Add the green beans and cook until just tender, about 2 minutes. Drain, run under cold water to stop the cooking, and set aside.

Remove the cardamom pods and bay leaf from the skillet and stir in the green beans and lamb. Continue to cook until the lamb is heated through, about 5 minutes. Season to taste with salt. Stir in the cashews and cilantro, sprinkle with the remaining ½ tsp. garam masala, and stir in the lemon juice. Serve immediately.

pork ragoût with soft polenta

This recipe is comfort on a plate; it's reason enough to make the slow-roasted pork in the first place. **Serves 4**

- 2 cups whole milk; more as needed

  Kosher salt
- 1 cup yellow stone-ground cornmeal
- ¼ cup freshly grated Parmigiano-Reggiano; more for sprinkling
- 1½ Tbs. unsalted butter
- 2 Tbs. extra-virgin olive oil
- 2 medium carrots, cut into small dice
- 2 medium ribs celery, cut into small dice
- 1 medium yellow onion, cut into small dice

  Pinch of crushed red pepper flakes
- 3 canned tomatoes, drained and cut into medium dice
- 3 cloves garlic, finely chopped
- 3 cups leftover shredded roast pork shoulder
- 3 cups lower-salt chicken broth

  Freshly ground black pepper
- 2 Tbs. chopped fresh flat-leaf parsley

Combine the milk with 2 cups water in a medium heavy-duty saucepan and bring to a boil over medium-high heat (watch carefully to prevent a boilover). Add 1½ tsp. salt and whisk in the cornmeal in a fine stream. Continue to whisk until the polenta begins to thicken, 1 to 3 minutes. Reduce the heat so that the polenta slowly bubbles and cook, uncovered, stirring frequently, until tender and no longer gritty, 20 to 40 minutes, depending on the cornmeal. If the polenta becomes too thick in the process, add milk, a little at a time, to maintain a soft consistency. When the polenta is done, stir in the Parmigiano and ½ Tbs. of the butter and season to taste with salt. Keep warm until serving. (The polenta will thicken as it sits. If necessary, add a splash of milk to thin it just before serving.)

Heat the oil in a 10-inch straight-sided sauté pan over medium heat. Add the carrots, celery, onion, pepper flakes, and a generous pinch of salt and cook, stirring often, until tender and starting to brown, 8 to 10 minutes. Add the tomatoes and garlic and cook, stirring, for another minute. Add the pork and chicken broth. Bring to a boil and then lower the heat to maintain a simmer. Cook until the broth has reduced by half, about 10 minutes. Stir in the remaining 1 Tbs. butter. Season to taste with salt and pepper.

Spoon the polenta into shallow bowls and then spoon the ragout on the top and to one side, with the broth pooling around the polenta. (Make sure each portion gets a fair share of broth.) Sprinkle each portion with parsley and Parmigiano and serve immediately.

pork and potato hash with poached eggs and avocado

Tender pork makes a nice change of pace for hash. **Serves 4**

- 1½ lb. russet potatoes, peeled and cut into small dice (about 3¾ cups)

  Kosher salt
- 2 Tbs. extra-virgin olive oil; more as needed
- 1 medium yellow onion, cut into small dice (about 1¼ cups)
- 2¼ cups leftover finely shredded roast pork shoulder
- 2 medium cloves garlic, finely chopped
- ½ tsp. white wine vinegar or lemon juice
- 4 large eggs
- 1 large ripe avocado, sliced
- ¼ cup coarsely chopped fresh cilantro

  Piment d'Espelette or other medium-hot red chile flakes, to taste (optional)

Put the potatoes in a medium saucepan, add water to cover by ¾ inch, and add 1 Tbs. salt. Bring to a boil, reduce the heat to maintain a simmer, and cook the potatoes until tender but not falling apart, about 5 minutes. Drain, transfer to a plate, and set aside.

Heat the oil in a 10-inch straight-sided sauté pan over medium-high heat. Add the onion and ½ tsp. salt and cook, stirring occasionally until soft, 5 to 7 minutes. Add the pork and continue to cook until the pork is warm, about 3 minutes. Add the garlic and cook, stirring, until the raw garlic aroma subsides, about 1 minute. Add the potatoes, toss to combine, and continue to cook, stirring, until heated through, 1 to 3 minutes more. Season to taste with salt. If the hash is a little dry, add a drizzle of olive oil. Keep warm.

Fill a medium saucepan with 3 inches of water. Add the vinegar and a pinch of salt; bring the water to a simmer. Crack the eggs one at a time into a small bowl and gently slide each into the water. Poach the eggs, gently turning once or twice until the whites are opaque but the yolks are still soft, 3 to 4 minutes. Using a slotted spoon, remove the eggs from the water and gently blot dry with a towel.

Evenly distribute the hash among four plates. Prop a poached egg and a few slices of avocado next to each portion. Sprinkle the egg and avocado with salt. Sprinkle the cilantro and piment d'Espelette (if using) over the hash, and serve immediately.

Roasted Strawberry Shortcakes
with Vanilla Biscuits, p. 120

Desserts

Roasted fruit makes sweet, tender, memorable treats.

the recipes

roasted strawberry shortcakes with vanilla biscuits

These vanilla biscuits are best fresh from the oven, so if you can, bake them about an hour before you plan to serve the shortcakes. The whipped cream in the biscuit dough is a bit unusual, and the results are out of this world. **Serves 6**

- 8 oz. (1¾ cups) unbleached all-purpose flour
- ½ cup plus 3 Tbs. granulated sugar; more for sprinkling
- 1 Tbs. baking powder
- ¼ tsp. table salt
- 1½ cups chilled heavy cream; more for brushing
- 2 tsp. pure vanilla extract
- 1¾ cups Roasted Strawberries (recipe below)
- ½ cup sour cream
- 2 Tbs. confectioners' sugar

Position a rack in the middle of the oven and heat the oven to 425°F. Grease a large baking sheet. In a large bowl, whisk the flour, 3 Tbs. of the sugar, the baking powder, and the salt.

In another large bowl, beat 1 cup of the cream with an electric mixer on medium-high speed just until the cream holds soft peaks when the beaters are lifted. Beat in the vanilla.

Make a well in the center of the flour mixture, add the whipped cream, and stir with a fork just until the mixture begins to hold together as dough. Turn the dough out onto a lightly floured surface and knead just until well combined, about six times. Pat the dough until it's about ½ inch thick. Cut out a total of six rounds with a 3-inch crinkle- or smooth-edged biscuit cutter, gathering the scraps and reshaping as needed. Lightly brush the tops of the rounds with cream and sprinkle with granulated sugar. Arrange the biscuits on the baking sheet. Bake until golden-brown, 12 to 15 minutes. Transfer with a spatula to a rack and let cool. Increase the oven temperature to 450°F and roast the strawberries as described below.

To serve, whip the remaining ½ cup cream with the sour cream and confectioners' sugar until it holds soft peaks when the beaters are lifted. Split each biscuit horizontally with a fork, lay a bottom half on each of six serving plates, and spoon over a portion of the warm roasted berries. Garnish with a dollop of cream, add the biscuit top, drizzle with the syrup from the roasted berries, and serve immediately.

> **Smaller berries have the best flavor; the huge ones, while striking, are often woolly and bland.**

roasted strawberries

As the strawberries roast, their juices thicken into a beautiful, sweet sauce.
Yields about 1¾ cups

- 1 qt. (about 1 lb.) small ripe fresh strawberries, hulled
- ½ cup granulated sugar

Position a rack in the middle of the oven and heat the oven to 450°F. Toss the strawberries in a bowl with the sugar. Transfer to a rimmed baking sheet. When the oven is hot, roast the strawberries, giving them a stir every 5 minutes, until they're soft and fragrant, about 15 minutes total. Transfer the baking sheet to a rack to cool for 5 minutes, then scrape the berries with their sauce into a small bowl. If using in ice cream sundaes, chill in the refrigerator until cold, about 2 hours, or up to a day.

roasted plantains with brown sugar and rum

These beg to be served with a scoop of vanilla or coconut ice cream on top. **Serves 4**

Butter or cooking spray for the pan

3 plantains, fully black and soft

¼ cup granulated sugar

2 Tbs. dark brown sugar

Large pinch ground cinnamon (optional)

2 Tbs. dark rum

2 Tbs. orange juice

2 Tbs. unsalted butter, cut into small pieces

Heat the oven to 375°F and grease an 8x8-inch baking dish with butter or cooking spray.

Trim the ends of the plantains and peel off the skin. Slice them on an angle to get ½-inch-thick oval slices. Layer the plantain slices in the baking dish so they overlap slightly. Sprinkle on both sugars and the cinnamon.

Drizzle the rum and orange juice over the plantains and dot the butter pieces on top. Bake until the plantains are golden-brown, tender, and have lost their shape a bit, 30 to 40 minutes. Let cool for at least 10 minutes. Serve warm or at room temperature.

roasted rhubarb granita

Most granitas are a combination of fruit purée and simple syrup. Here, a pinch of salt and a little lemon juice bring out the flavor and balance the sweetness.

Makes about 5 cups

2 lb. rhubarb stalks, washed, trimmed, and cut into 1-in. pieces

1 cinnamon stick

1 3-in. branch rosemary

1 Tbs. fresh lemon juice

Pinch of salt

1 cup simple syrup (at right)

Put the rhubarb in a nonreactive baking dish with the cinnamon and rosemary. Sprinkle with the lemon juice and add a pinch of salt.

Cover with aluminum foil and roast in a 375°F oven for 40 minutes, or until the rhubarb is soft. Remove the cinnamon stick and rosemary.

Purée the rhubarb, combine with the simple syrup, and freeze.

roasting rhubarb

Some fruits need cooking to release their flavors and to soften their textures. Roasting rhubarb with cinnamon sticks and rosemary softens and flavors the fruit.

SIMPLE SYRUP
To sweeten this granita, you'll need a simple syrup. To make it, just bring an equal volume of sugar and water to a boil and cook, stirring, just until the sugar is dissolved. Let cool off the heat and refrigerate for up to a month.

sugar-roasted peaches

Sprinkling peaches with sugar and roasting them makes them sweeter still, while bacon and herbs add a bit of welcome savory flavor. If you want to make them vegetarian-friendly, omit the bacon and use extra-virgin olive oil instead. Serve the peaches simply with a dollop of plain Greek yogurt or a scoop of ice cream for a snack or light dessert, or try them in the recipe on p. 124.

Yields 8 peach halves

- 2 **slices thick-cut bacon**
- 4 **ripe semi-firm medium peaches (about 8 oz. each), halved and pitted**
- 2 **tsp. raw sugar, such as demerara or turbinado**

  Kosher salt and freshly ground black pepper
- 3 **large sprigs fresh summer or winter savory, thyme, or rosemary**

Position a rack in the center of the oven and heat the oven to 450°F.

Cook the bacon in a 12-inch cast-iron skillet over medium heat, flipping occasionally, until crisp, 5 to 8 minutes. Drain on a plate lined with paper towels. Pour the bacon fat from the skillet into a small heatproof bowl, leaving a slick of fat in the skillet; you'll need 4 tsp. reserved fat. (If you don't have enough, make up the difference with extra-virgin olive oil.) Raise the heat under the skillet to medium high.

Sprinkle the cut sides of the peaches evenly with the sugar and a tiny pinch each of salt **1** and pepper. Arrange the peaches in the skillet cut side down and tuck the herbs around them **2**. Tear the bacon slices in quarters and tuck the pieces around the peaches. Drizzle 2 tsp. of the reserved bacon fat evenly over the peaches and let them cook undisturbed until the cut sides begin to brown **3**, about 5 minutes.

Sprinkle the uncut sides of the peaches with a tiny pinch of salt, then transfer the skillet to the oven and roast until the peaches are just tender, about 10 minutes.

Flip the peaches, drizzle with 2 tsp. more of the reserved bacon fat **4**, and continue to roast until they're tender but not falling apart, about 5 minutes more. Enjoy the bacon as a cook's treat, or save it for another use; discard the herbs. Let the peaches cool slightly before serving.

You can make the peaches up to 2 days ahead and refrigerate them in an airtight container. To reheat, arrange the peaches on a microwave-safe dish, cover loosely with a paper towel, and heat on high for about 1 minute.

choose fragrant peaches and use them fast

Here's a great motto when choosing peaches: If they smell good, they'll taste good. It's great to buy peaches at your local farmers' market, but you can find good ones in many grocery stores as well. Look for unblemished peaches that aren't too soft. When you have perfectly ripe peaches, enjoy them within a couple of days. Don't wash them until you're ready to use them or they're likely to develop mold.

Occasionally, imperfect peaches may be all that's available. If they're underripe, you can ripen them by simply leaving them out on the counter and turning them daily so they're evenly exposed to light and air.

how to sugar-roast

Sprinkling the halved peaches with raw sugar and kosher salt draws out moisture and boosts the caramelization process in the skillet.

Don't crowd the peaches in the skillet or they may steam instead of sear. You also want to leave room for fresh herb sprigs and pieces of bacon, which add great flavor.

Resist the urge to move the peaches during the first 5 minutes of cooking so the cut sides have a chance to caramelize. Then check their undersides—when they begin to brown, it's time to put the skillet in the oven.

After about 10 minutes of roasting, the cut sides will be deeply browned, but the peaches won't be fully tender. Flip them at this point so the cut sides don't burn, drizzle with a bit more fat, and return them to the oven to finish cooking.

sugar-roasted peach and cornbread sundaes with bacon syrup

Here, cakey cornbread is paired with the smoky-sweet peaches, salty bacon-studded maple syrup, and rich vanilla gelato. A sprinkle of fruity Aleppo pepper (see Test Kitchen, p. 129, for more information) and minced fresh sage completes the sweet-salty-spicy-herbal equation. **Serves 8, with leftover cornbread**

FOR THE CORNBREAD

- 8 Tbs. unsalted butter, softened; more for the baking dish
- 9 oz. (2 cups) unbleached all-purpose flour; more for the baking dish
- 3 oz. (½ cup) fine yellow cornmeal
- 2 tsp. baking powder
- ¾ tsp. kosher salt
- 1 cup granulated sugar
- 3 large eggs, at room temperature
- ½ cup heavy cream
- ½ cup whole milk
- ½ cup sour cream

FOR THE BACON SYRUP

- 6 slices thick-cut bacon, preferably applewood-smoked
- ¾ cup pure maple syrup
- ¼ cup honey

FOR SERVING

- 8 Sugar-Roasted Peach halves, warmed (recipe, p. 122)

Make Ahead

The syrup can be made up to 5 days ahead and refrigerated. Warm over low heat before using. The cornbread can be made up to 1 day ahead; wrap and store at room temperature.

Vanilla gelato or ice cream
Minced fresh sage, for garnish
Aleppo pepper flakes, for garnish (optional)

MAKE THE CORNBREAD

Position a rack in the center of the oven and heat the oven to 375°F. Butter and flour an 8-inch square baking dish.

In a large bowl, whisk the flour, cornmeal, baking powder, and salt. Set aside.

In a stand mixer fitted with the paddle attachment or in a large bowl with a handheld electric mixer, beat the butter and sugar on medium speed until light and fluffy, about 2 minutes. Gradually beat in the eggs, one at a time, until well combined. Adjust the mixer speed to low and add the cream, milk, and sour cream; mix until combined. The batter may look curdled at this point. Add the dry ingredients, mixing until just combined and scraping down the sides as needed. Pour the batter into the prepared baking dish, smooth the top, and firmly tap the dish on the counter to break any air bubbles.

Bake until a toothpick inserted in the center comes out clean, about 40 minutes. Let the cornbread cool in its dish on a rack until warm. (The cornbread can be made up to 1 day ahead; wrap tightly and store at room temperature.)

MAKE THE BACON SYRUP

In a 12-inch skillet, cook the bacon over medium heat, flipping occasionally, until crisp, 5 to 8 minutes. Transfer to paper towels to drain and then coarsely chop. Pour off all but 1 Tbs. of the fat from the skillet.

Add the maple syrup and honey to the skillet and heat over medium heat, stirring to combine. Return the bacon to the skillet and stir to combine and heat through, about 5 minutes. Remove the skillet from the heat and let the syrup cool to warm.

SERVE

Cut eight 2-inch cubes from the cornbread (you'll have leftover cornbread). If made ahead, warm the cubes in a 250°F oven for 10 minutes, or lightly toast them in a toaster oven. Put a cube of cornbread on each of eight plates. Arrange the peaches and scoops of gelato near the cornbread. Top with the bacon syrup, sage, and a tiny pinch of Aleppo pepper, if using.

roasted red grapes with mascarpone and rum

You can use any grape variety in this 15-minute dessert, though some types will collapse and get juicy more quickly than others. Adjust the baking time as needed.

Serves 4

- 1 lb. seedless red grapes, left on the stems and cut into small clusters
- 4 tsp. honey
- 1 tsp. extra-virgin olive oil
- ½ tsp. flaky sea salt
- ½ cup mascarpone
- 1½ Tbs. regular or spiced dark rum
- 1 tsp. finely grated orange zest

Position a rack in the center of the oven and heat the oven to 475°F.

In a large bowl, gently toss the grape clusters, 2 tsp. of the honey, the oil, and the salt. Spread the grapes on a large rimmed baking sheet in a single layer and roast, flipping halfway through, until collapsed, juicy, and somewhat caramelized, about 15 minutes.

Meanwhile, stir together the mascarpone, rum, zest, and remaining 2 tsp. honey in a medium bowl.

Transfer the roasted grapes to serving dishes and serve warm, with a dollop of the sweetened mascarpone.

test kitchen

TIPS/TECHNIQUES/INGREDIENTS

Cutting a large squash is a cinch with this four-step method.

How to cut a large squash

To make the **Roasted Hubbard Squash Soup with Hazelnuts and Chives** on p. 5, you'll need to cut up a very large squash. Here's a good way:

1

2

Prick the squash several times with a fork and microwave for 3 minutes; it will soften slightly, making it easier to cut open. Or bake the whole squash directly on the rack in a 350°F oven until slightly softened and the skin begins to change color, about 10 minutes. Set the squash on a towel on a cutting board to prevent it from slipping, and push the tip of a sharp chef's knife into the squash near the stem. Carefully push the knife through the squash to the cutting board to cut off the stem.

Then cut lengthwise through half of the squash, starting with the tip of your knife in the center of the squash. If the knife sticks, don't try to pull it out; this is dangerous, since it may come out suddenly. Instead, tap the handle with a rubber mallet or meat tenderizer until the knife cuts through the squash.

3

Rotate the squash and cut through the other side the same way.

shopping for hubbard squash

If buying a whole hubbard squash, choose one that feels heavy for its size with a matte (not glossy) skin. If buying in pieces, choose those with a deep orange flesh that looks firm and fresh-cut.

< 4 **Push the halves apart** with your hands. With a soup spoon, scrape the seeds and stringy bits away from the flesh and discard.

Piment d'Espelette

Though you could use regular cayenne or chile flakes to garnish the **Pork and Potato Hash** on p. 116, piment d'Espelette gives the dish an unusual Basque twist.

Piment d'Espelette chiles come from a group of ten villages (one of which is called Espelette) in the Basque region of southwestern France. After harvesting, the chiles are strung together and dried outside houses and shops in the villages—the image of a chile-festooned building is in the logo used to designate this product.

The slightly sweet, mildly spicy chiles are most commonly ground into a coarse powder. In the Basque region, the spice is often used in place of black pepper. In addition to using it as a finishing touch on dishes, try it in spice rubs and sauces.

Piment d'Espelette is available at specialty markets and by mail order. Store as you would any other spice: in an airtight container in a cool, dry place for up to six months.

Yuzu kosho

This spicy-tart Japanese condiment is featured in the **Lemon-Garlic Roast Chicken** on p. 48. It's made from the zest of yuzu—an aromatic Asian citrus fruit—mixed with minced chiles and salt. There are two kinds: green and red. The spicier and more common green yuzu kosho is made from unripe green yuzu zest and green chiles, while the milder, brighter red version is made from ripe yellow yuzu zest and red chiles. You can find both varieties in Asian markets and online. Yuzu kosho will keep, refrigerated in an airtight container, for up to 3 months.

More ways to use it

- Add it to soups at the end of cooking.

- Spread it over cooked steaks, pork chops, or meaty fish fillets.

- Dab it on steamed or baked sweet potatoes or roasted root vegetables.

- Mix it with ponzu for a dipping sauce for dumplings or cold noodles, or mix with soy sauce for a dipping sauce for sushi or sashimi.

- Use it to add citrus and spice flavors to vinaigrettes.

Orange slices and segments

Many recipes call for orange slices and/or segments, like the **Sear-Roasted Halibut with Blood Orange Salsa** on p. 34. Here's how to make them:

Cut off the top and bottom of the orange, slicing off enough to expose a circle of the orange's flesh.

With a paring knife, slice off a strip of peel from top to bottom. Try to get all of the white pith, but leave as much of the flesh as possible. Continue all the way around.

To make segments (a.k.a. suprêmes), use a paring knife to cut on either side of each membrane, freeing the orange segment in between. Work over a bowl to catch the juice.

To make slices, cut the orange crosswise to the desired thickness.

How to carve a ham

The **Fresh Ham with Rosemary, Garlic, and Lemon** on p. 92 is an impressive-looking roast, so you'll want to carve it at the table for the maximum wow-factor. Here's how to tackle it:

1

Put the ham on a carving board, positioning it on its widest side for stability. Start at the large end and use a long, sharp carving knife to cut thin slices perpendicular to the bone.

2

After cutting several slices, run the knife parallel to the bone to cut them free. Finish carving that section of the ham and then turn it and slice another side. Repeat.

Making gravy for a brined bird

A **wet-brined or dry-brined turkey** (like the one on p. 57) is more flavorful than an unbrined turkey, but the technique has one major drawback: salty pan juices. Pan juices are usually the backbone of turkey gravy, but gravy made only with the juices from a brined bird is bound to come out too salty. Fortunately, there's a solution to this problem: Make the gravy with plain turkey broth and use the pan juices judiciously as a seasoning. The recipe below illustrates this approach, which can be used for any wet- or dry-brined bird.

herb gravy for a brined turkey

Yields about 3½ cups

FOR THE TURKEY BROTH

	Turkey neck, gizzard, tail, and heart
2	Tbs. vegetable oil
1	large yellow onion, cut into 2-inch chunks
1	small carrot, peeled and cut into 2-inch pieces
1	celery stalk, cut into 2-inch pieces
1	bay leaf
2	large sprigs each fresh thyme and parsley
10	black peppercorns

FOR THE GRAVY

	Drippings from a roasted brined turkey (like the one on p. 57)
6	Tbs. unbleached all-purpose flour
1	tsp. chopped fresh sage (save the stems)
½	tsp. chopped fresh thyme (save the stems)
½	tsp. fresh lemon juice
	Freshly ground black pepper

MAKE THE BROTH

Chop the turkey neck into 3 or 4 pieces with a cleaver. Chop the gizzard in half. Heat the oil in a large saucepan over medium-low heat. Add the neck, gizzard, tail, and heart (do not use the liver) along with the onion. Stir to coat with oil, cover, and cook gently, stirring occasionally, for 20 minutes. The meat will begin releasing lots of juice.

Add 4 cups cold water and the carrot, celery, herbs, and peppercorns. Bring to a boil over medium-high heat, cover, and reduce the heat to maintain a gentle simmer. Simmer until the broth is flavorful, 30 to 40 minutes. Strain the broth and set aside until the fat rises to the top. Skim off and discard the fat. Use the broth immediately or cool and refrigerate for up to 3 days or freeze for up to 3 months.

MAKE THE GRAVY

Heat the giblet broth until hot. Pour the drippings from the roasting pan into a heatproof measuring cup or fat separator. Allow the fat to rise to the top and then spoon 4 Tbs. back into the roasting pan. Separate and discard the remaining fat from the pan juices. Season the giblet broth with the pan juices, adding only enough to make the broth very flavorful but not too salty. If necessary, add water until you have 4 cups of liquid.

Place the roasting pan over two burners set on medium heat. Sprinkle the flour into the pan and use a flat whisk or wooden spoon to combine it with the fat. Cook for about 2 minutes.

To keep lumps from forming in the gravy, slowly pour about ½ cup of the broth mixture into the pan while whisking vigorously to disperse the flour evenly into the liquid. The liquid should thicken quickly and get gluey. As soon as it thickens, add another ½ cup or so of broth while whisking. Repeat until the gravy starts looking more like a smooth sauce than glue. At this point, you can whisk in the remaining broth and bring the gravy to a simmer. Add the reserved herb stems and simmer for about 5 minutes to develop the flavors. Strain the gravy through a medium sieve, add the sage, thyme, and lemon juice, and season to taste with pepper.

Aleppo pepper

Aleppo pepper, which brings a fruity heat to the **Sugar-Roasted Peach and Corn-bread Sundaes with Bacon Syrup** on p. 124, comes from northern Syria, near the town of Aleppo, considered one of the culinary meccas of the Mediterranean. It's crushed from Halaby peppers (also called Halab or Near Eastern peppers), which have been naturally sun-dried for weeks and seeded.

Aleppo pepper is moderately hot and has a rich flavor that's similar to that of ancho chiles but with more heat and hints of cumin. It's great for seasoning anything from grilled meats to pizza to potatoes.

Boning turkey thighs and a breast

Turkey thighs and whole breasts are most often sold bone-in and skin-on, so if you're making the **Turkey Thighs Stuffed with Porcini, Sausage, and Artichoke Hearts** on p. 50 or the **Roasted Turkey Breast, Porchetta-Style** on p. 52, you'll probably need to sharpen your boning knife and remove some bones. It's not hard, once you know the techniques. Just follow these steps:

BONING
THE THIGH

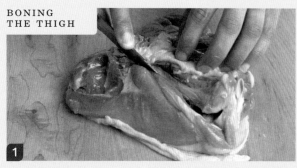

1

Put a thigh skin side down on a cutting board. Using a boning knife, begin cutting between the thigh bone and the meat as close to the bone as possible.

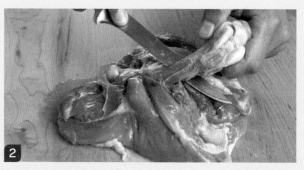

2

Continue to work your knife around the bone and thigh joint, making sure that no gristle or cartilage remains attached to the meat, until the bone is cut completely free.

BONING
THE BREAST

1

Lay the breast skin side down on a cutting board. If the backbone is still attached to the breast, cut it away with poultry shears. Next, locate the wish bone in the V-shaped neck end of the breast. Using a boning knife, scrape the meat away from the bone and remove the bone.

2

Remove the rib cage and breast bone by cutting between the ribs and the meat at one edge of the breast. Scrape the knife as close to the rib bones as possible, and as the bones come free, pull back on them to make cutting between the bones and meat easier. Continue until you reach the breast bone.

3

Scrape the point of the knife along the breast bone and use your thumb to free the meat. Be careful not to cut through the meat and skin at the ridge of the breast bone (the meat is very thin here).

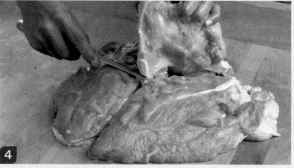

4

Once you bone half the breast, scrape along the other side of the breast bone and along the ribs until the entire rib cage and breast bone can be freed in one piece.

3 ways to toast pine nuts

Heat releases and intensifies the rich flavor of pine nuts, which is why the **Pork Chops Stuffed with Pine Nuts and Herbs** recipe on p. 101 calls for toasted nuts. There are three ways to go about toasting the nuts, each with its own pros and cons:

OVEN
Spread the nuts on a baking sheet and bake at 375°F, stirring occasionally, until golden-brown, 5 to 10 minutes.
Pro: The color of oven-toasted nuts is evenly golden.
Con: You have to heat the oven. We tend to use this method only if we're heating the oven for other reasons, too.

TOASTER OVEN
Spread the nuts on the baking sheet that came with the toaster oven and bake at 325°F, stirring frequently, until golden-brown, 3 to 5 minutes.
Pro: Produces results similar to those from a conventional oven, but a toaster oven heats up much faster and is more energy-efficient.
Con: Closer proximity to the heating elements in a toaster oven increases the risk of burning the nuts, hence the need for more frequent stirring and a lower baking temperature.

SKILLET
Put the nuts in a dry skillet and cook over medium-low heat, stirring frequently, until golden in spots, about 3 minutes.
Pro: The quickest and most convenient method.
Con: The nuts develop spotty, uneven color and burn more easily than with the two oven methods.

TOASTER OVEN

SKILLET

OVEN

Lamb leg lingo

Whole legs of lamb in the United States tend to run as large as 8 pounds, which is more than many people need. For this reason, they're often halved before sale; the **Rosemary-Garlic Roast Leg of Lamb** on p. 86 calls for the shank half. Here's how the halves compare:

SHANK HALF
This is the thigh from the hind leg. Meaty at the top and becoming narrower toward the knee, this cut is lean and easy to carve.

BUTT HALF
This is the hip and rump. Though this cut, which includes the sirloin, is tender, it's hard to carve. When it's bone-in, it may include the hip—or aitch—bone, which can be awkward to work around.

TIP

Give your turkey a rest before and after roasting

For the juiciest turkey, allow the bird to sit for about an hour at room temperature before roasting. This time out of the refrigerator allows the internal temperature of the meat to reach 165°F sooner as it roasts, before the outside of the turkey becomes dry. The muscle fibers also relax after being cold for so long, which results in meat that's more tender.

The turkey also needs to rest after roasting and before carving so its juice, forced to the center by the heat, is redistributed back into the meat. While it's resting, though, some juice will inevitably run onto the carving board, which can be messy if you don't have a board with a deep trench. We solved this problem by putting a paper towel ring around the turkey. To make one, start with a four- or five-sheet length of paper towels and scrunch it into a snake. Wrap it around the base of the turkey and it will soak up that wayward juice and make cleanup a snap.

INGREDIENT

Farro

Cultivated in Italy for centuries, farro (FAHR-ro) is an ancient variety of wheat. Also known as emmer, it has a high protein and fiber content and a nutty, chewy texture that's great in grain salads like the **Roasted Broccoli and Farro Salad with Feta** on p. 13. It's also delicious in soups, stuffings, and pilafs. Farro (*triticum dicoccum*) is often confused with spelt (*triticum spelta*), but they're different species of wheat.

Like common wheat, farro is available in various forms. It's ground into flour, which can be used to make pasta, baked goods, and even roux. It's also cracked, like bulgur. Or you can buy the grains whole, semi-pearled, or pearled, all of which are options for the farro salad.

Semi-pearled and pearled farro cook faster than whole-grain farro (30 minutes versus 60 minutes), but the trade-off is decreased nutritional content. Pearling removes the inedible hull that surrounds the grain, but the process also scours off part (semi-pearled) or all (pearled) of the nutritious germ and bran. Whole-grain farro is hulled using a gentler process that leaves the germ and bran intact. Store pearled farro in the freezer for up to 6 months after opening; whole-grain farro will keep in a cupboard almost indefinitely.

How to prep roast pork with crisp crackling

A pork loin roast topped with shatteringly crisp crackling is irresistible. The crackling comes from the layer of skin and fat that naturally tops a pig's loin muscle; when roasted, it renders into a deliciously crisp, bubbly crust. The fat bastes the meat as it cooks, too, for juicy, tender results. (See the **Roast Pork with Crisp Crackling and Red Currant Gravy** recipe on p. 105.) You'll need to pre-order the roast to include the skin and fat and then do a little prep work at home.

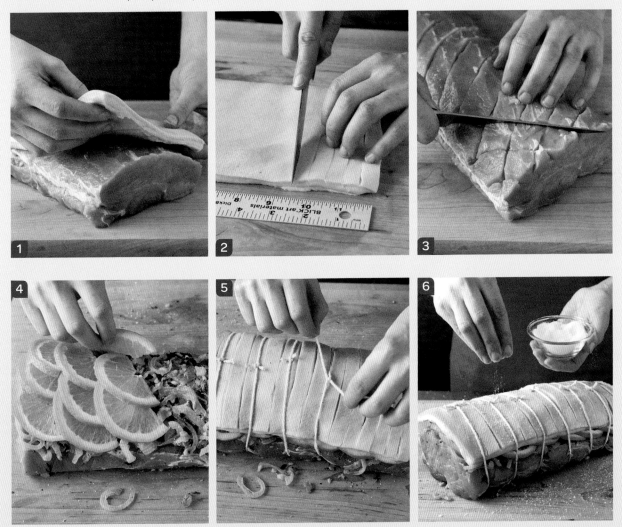

1. Ask your butcher to remove the skin and fat from the pork loin roast in one piece, trim the fat down to about ¼ inch thick, and then set it back on top of the roast; this is what it should look like. **2.** At home, remove the fat and skin layer and score the skin crosswise through to the fat in ½-inch intervals. The score marks will make it easier to carve the roast later. **3.** Score the meat in a crosshatch pattern, cutting about ½ inch deep, to help the seasonings penetrate the meat. **4.** Season the meat generously with salt and pepper and then top with the sautéed onions and the orange slices. **5.** Lay the skin and fat back over the oranges and tie the roast at 1½-inch intervals with kitchen twine. **6.** Generously season the skin with salt, and then roast according to the recipe.

red-wine chicken stock

This chicken stock is used as the base for the Red Currant Gravy on p. 105. It has a robust chicken flavor with added acidity and earthiness from the wine and celery root. The recipe makes more than needed for the gravy; freeze the extra in ice cube trays and use to deglaze pans for sauces. **Yields 4 cups**

- **4** Tbs. salted or unsalted butter
- **1** 3-lb. chicken, quartered
- **1** small celery root (about 10 oz.), peeled and cut into 1-inch pieces
- **1** medium yellow onion (with peel), quartered
- **2** cups dry red wine, such as Pinot Noir or Cabernet Sauvignon
- **10** sprigs fresh thyme
- **1** Tbs. black peppercorns
- **1** Tbs. kosher salt

Melt the butter in an 8-quart stockpot over medium heat. Add the chicken and cook, turning once, until browned, about 12 minutes. Add the remaining ingredients and enough water to just cover the chicken (about 7 cups). Bring to a boil, then turn the heat down and simmer, uncovered, skimming off any foam, until the broth is flavorful, about 2½ hours.

Strain into a large container, pressing on the solids to extract as much liquid as possible (discard the solids). Let cool. Cover the stock and refrigerate for up to 2 days or freeze for up to 6 months. Skim off and discard any fat before using.

Ways to use duck and goose fat

A nice little bonus comes out of roasting duck and goose: lots of rendered duck and goose fat, a tasty alternative to oil and butter. Stored in the freezer, it'll last for up to a year. Because the duck fat from the recipe on p. 66 is subtly flavored with tangerine zest and five-spice powder, it's best used in Asian or North African styles of cooking, like stir-fries or tagines. The goose fat on p. 68 is plain and therefore more versatile. Here are some of our favorite ways to use it (these ideas will work with unflavored duck fat, too, if you happen to have some):

Roasted potatoes Toss baby red potato wedges with 1 Tbs. fat, salt, and pepper. Roast in a hot oven until tender, and then sprinkle with fresh thyme.

Sautéed baby carrots and cipollini onions Sauté peeled baby carrots and cipollini onions in 1 Tbs. fat with a little honey and a pinch of cayenne until tender and browned.

Fennel confit Poach wedges of fennel in enough fat to cover until meltingly tender; serve alongside steak or lamb chops.

Sole meunière Dredge four sole fillets in flour. Pan-sear in 2 Tbs. fat until golden-brown on both sides and cooked through. Sprinkle with lemon juice and parsley.

Warm vinaigrette Warm 3 Tbs. fat and gradually whisk it into 1 Tbs. red-wine vinegar and ¼ tsp. Dijon mustard. Add chopped shallot and tarragon. Toss with spinach or frisée.

Chive and goose fat biscuits Substitute cold fat for the butter in your favorite biscuit recipe and add chopped chives with the liquid ingredients.

For juicier meat, give it a rest

Most roast recipes call for letting the cooked meat rest before carving. Here's why:

When meat is cooked with dry heat (like roasting), the cells in the muscles soften and contract, releasing liquid, most of which is forced by the heat toward the cooler center of the meat. If you were to cut into the meat right after cooking, all the juice would pool onto your cutting board, leaving you with meat that's dry.

But if the meat rests, it begins to cool slightly and the process is reversed: The juice is able to flow back into the outer muscle fibers, where it stays during carving, making the meat juicy throughout.

How long a piece of meat needs to rest depends on its thickness. A 1-inch-thick steak or chop will need about 5 minutes to rest, whereas a large roast benefits from 30 minutes to an hour.

UNRESTED

If meat is sliced right after cooking, the juice runs out from the center, leaving the meat dry.

RESTED

The juice has had time to be redistributed throughout the meat so it stays inside when the meat is sliced.

Roast beef companion

The beef rib roast recipe on p. 88 has a classic companion, Yorkshire pudding. Similar in texture and flavor to a popover, Yorkshire pudding is made with the delicious fat from the drippings left in the roasting pan. To make it without a roast, you can substitute melted butter or bacon fat for the beef fat. **Serves 8**

yorkshire pudding

1½ **cups whole milk**
3 **large eggs**
   Kosher salt
6¾ **oz. (1½ cups) unbleached all-purpose flour**
6 **Tbs. rendered beef fat**

Position a rack in the lower third of the oven and heat the oven to 450°F.
In a medium bowl, whisk together the milk, eggs, and ½ tsp. salt until smooth. Whisk in the flour just until incorporated; the batter will be lumpy.
Pour the fat into a metal 9x13-inch baking pan and put the pan in the oven until hot, about 5 minutes.
Remove the pan from the oven and pour the batter into the hot fat. Bake until puffed and browned, about 20 minutes. Serve immediately.

How to peel pearl onions

It's almost as if pearl onions don't want to be peeled. Their tiny size and tightly wrapped skin make handling them awkward. And if you sacrifice the more easily peeled first fleshy layer, it doesn't leave you with much onion.

The easiest way to peel just the pearl onion's outer skin is by blanching in boiling water. To do this, bring a small saucepan of water to a boil and fill a medium bowl with ice water. Trim both ends of each onion and put them in the boiling water for about 30 seconds. Then transfer the onions to the ice water to stop the cooking. Once they're cool, use a paring knife to slip off the skins.

Test fish for doneness like a pro

Restaurant chefs have an ingenious way of checking whether a piece of fish is properly cooked without having to cut it open, and it's something home cooks can easily do, too. Simply plunge a small sharp knife all the way through the thickest part of a fish fillet and hold it there for 5 seconds. Pull it out and carefully touch the flat side of the knife to your lower lip, which is very sensitive to temperature. If it feels warm, the fish is just cooked through and ready to serve. If the knife is still cold or cool, the fish needs more time.

Use aluminum foil shiny side up or down

Most people think it matters whether aluminum foil is used shiny side up or down, but the surprising truth is that it doesn't make a difference. The variation is a result of the manufacturing process—the shiny side comes in contact with highly polished steel rollers, and the matte side doesn't. The appearance has no effect on how the foil performs.

Slicing an onion

When you slice an onion, you want to cut the pieces into similar widths so they cook evenly. To do this, slice the onion at an angle, following its natural curve, rather than slicing it straight down, which yields wider end pieces.

Peel and halve the onion from end to end; then notch out the root end of each half so the slices will separate as you cut them.

1

Holding your knife at a low angle, start cutting thin lengthwise slices on one side of the onion. Following the natural curve of the onion, adjust the angle of the knife as you slice. The knife should be at 90 degrees when you reach the middle of the onion.

2

Once you get to the middle, flip the onion over and repeat.

3

What we mean by dice

To "dice" means to cut a food into cubes, making it look like playing dice—hence the name. If the food is flat, like a bell pepper, the dice will be more of a square than a cube. Each size of dice has its own corresponding measurement, as shown at right. That said, there's no need to pull a ruler out every time. Use these dimensions as guidelines, and try to keep the dice a consistent size so the food cooks evenly.

Large dice = ¾ inch

Medium dice = ⅓ to ½ inch

Small dice = ¼ inch

Fine dice = ⅛ inch

Roasting meat 101

Roasts can seem mysterious. Cuts of meat vary widely in thickness and in protein, water, and fat content, all of which can change the ideal roasting method. And when you're roasting, all of the cooking happens out of plain sight. But in truth, roasting meat is very simple—once you know what's going on behind that closed oven door.

Why do roasting recipes say to let the meat stand at room temperature for up to an hour before cooking?

To take the chill off the meat's surface so it browns better. Meat is typically refrigerated at about 37°F, but browning doesn't begin to occur until about 310°F. Letting meat sit out gradually raises the meat's surface temperature, so when it hits the hot oven, it quickly reaches browning temperature and develops a thick crust. (Cold meat won't brown as quickly or as easily.) Small roasts (less than 3 pounds) will lose their surface chill in less than 30 minutes, while large roasts can rest for up to an hour. (For food safety, the meat shouldn't sit out for more than 2 hours.)

Should I roast meat on or off the bone?

If you have a choice between a boneless roast and one that's bone-in, go for the bone-in. Bone-in roasts taste juicier and richer, thanks to collagen, a type of fibrous protein that concentrates in bones and in the cartilage surrounding bones. During cooking, water in the meat is driven out of the cells, helping to dissolve the collagen in and around the bone into rich-tasting gelatin, which creates a better mouthfeel.

Roasting meat on the bone also produces tender, rare meat near the bone (hence the phrase "tender at the bone"). That's because the honeycomb air pockets in bones make poor conductors of heat. Bones slow down the cooking, causing meat near the bone to roast at a slower rate and remain more rare.

Is it better to roast meat at a high heat quickly or at a low heat slowly?

It all depends on the cut of meat you're roasting and the results you want. Roasting at high temperatures (400°F and above) browns meat quickly, which makes a roast look and taste delicious. This method is generally best for thin, tender cuts like beef and pork tenderloin, which rely on that well-browned crust for flavor. But high heat also has a drawback—it can cause moisture loss, resulting in drier meat.

For thick and somewhat tender cuts like beef standing rib roasts and center-cut pork loin roasts, a moderated version of high-temperature roasting works best. With this method, you start the meat roasting at a high temperature (450°F to 500°F) to brown the surface, and then reduce the heat to a more moderate temperature (300°F to 350°F), so the meat can gradually reach the ideal internal temperature. Some cooks prefer to do the browning step in a hot pan on the stovetop and then transfer the meat to a 300°F to 350°F oven to finish roasting. This stovetop-to-oven method works best with smaller roasts, like rack of lamb.

Finally, low-temperature roasting (below 250°F) is excellent for very large and/or tough cuts of meat like pork shoulder and beef chuck roast. Lowering the temperature may limit the degree of flavorful surface browning, but it allows the meat to cook more evenly from the surface to the interior. Low heat also helps keep the entire roast moist, which reduces shrinkage and improves juiciness. Most important, slow-roasting allows time for the collagen to dissolve into gelatin, and for enzymes in the meat to help break

down and tenderize the tough fibers, resulting in a more succulent texture.

Why should meat rest after roasting?

To make it juicier. During roasting, the heat concentrates the juices in the center of the meat. If you cut into it straight out of the oven, the juices readily dribble onto the plate. But as the meat cools, the proteins become firmer and are better able to retain the juices.

Keep in mind that, early on in the resting period, the heat from the surface of the roast will continue to radiate toward the center, causing the internal temperature to rise a few degrees at a rate relative to the meat's density and thickness. This is called carryover cooking. For this reason, roasted meats—especially large or thick roasts and those roasted at high temperatures—should be removed from the heat when they are 5°F to 15°F shy of the desired internal temperature, depending on the roast's size and the type of meat. (Note that good recipes should take this into account, instructing you to remove meat from the oven before it reaches the desired doneness temperature.) For an accurate temperature reading, insert the thermometer into the thickest part of the meat but not near or touching bone. Bones conduct heat more slowly than do fat and muscle, so meat near the bone will register a slightly lower temperature.

How long you let the meat rest depends on the size and final internal temperature of the roast. Meat tends to taste best eaten at a temperature of about 120°F. The larger the roast and the higher the meat's final temperature, the longer it will take for the internal temperature to drop to 120°F.

dry heat

When we roast or bake, we surround food with hot, dry air (300° to 500°F), which heats the surface, evaporates moisture, and allows browning to occur. It takes much longer to roast or bake food than to sear or sauté it because air is a poor heat conductor (you've probably noticed that you can put your hand in a 400°F oven but not in 400°F oil or in boiling water). This makes roasting ideal for cooking large cuts of meat or whole vegetables.

Roasting pans 101

The biggest meals of the year always seem to revolve around a roasted something—a turkey, a rib roast, a leg of lamb—and using a good-quality roasting pan is essential for great results. So what defines a good-quality pan? It needs to be able to withstand hot oven temperatures as well as the direct heat from a stovetop burner (for making gravies and sauces from pan drippings) without warping or buckling. To do that, it should be made of multiple layers of metal, usually aluminum (which is a good conductor of heat) and stainless steel (which is durable and nonreactive); this construction is known as "tri-ply," "five-ply," or "clad."

Tri-ply roasting pans aren't cheap, usually costing at least $100. For a holiday like Thanksgiving, though, when the goal is a perfectly browned bird and deeply flavorful gravy, the price is entirely worth it. Plus, you can use your pan for so much more throughout the year, such as roasted vegetables, lasagne, casseroles, braises, or water baths for custards and cheesecakes.

WHAT TO CONSIDER

- **Material:** Look for pans labeled tri-ply, five-ply, or clad. These are less likely to warp or buckle at high temperatures. Opt for one with a stainless-steel (not nonstick) interior, as it will promote better browning.

- **Weight:** A pan should weigh between 5 and 6 pounds. An empty 8-pound pan may not seem heavy, but with a rack and a turkey, it'll be a chore to lug in and out of the oven. Pans that are less than 5 pounds often buckle and warp.

- **Handles:** Vertical handles are the safest and provide the most stability. Horizontal handles stick out and may not fit inside all ovens. Handles should be at least 4 inches wide—any narrower and it'll be hard to get a good grip.

- **Sides:** While sloped sides are more whisk-friendly, vertical sides create a larger cooking area; select whichever works best for you. All pans should have generously rounded corners, so you can reach every inch while stirring. In terms of height, shorter sides may promote a bit more browning, since more of the roast is exposed to the oven's heat, but add a rack to any pan, and side height becomes a moot point.

- **Shape:** As a general rule, go with a rectangular pan. Oval roasters, which usually have less surface area, are limiting.

HOW TO CHOOSE A ROASTING RACK

A roasting rack lifts food off the bottom of the pan. This keeps a roast away from its drippings, exposes more of it to the oven's heat for better browning, creates room underneath for aromatics and vegetables, and makes removing the roast from the pan much easier. Many roasting pans come with a rack, but don't assume they're all created equal. If yours doesn't meet the following criteria, consider buying a new rack; they usually cost less than $20.

Handles should be at least 4 inches wide and positioned on the long sides of the rack so they don't interfere with the roasting pan's handles; this allows for the easiest roast removal.

Racks should be V- or U-shaped. These cradle and stabilize a roast, while leaving enough room beneath for aromatics or vegetables. Flat racks provide much less support and are harder to remove.

TIP

Cut the fat

A fat separator is a handy tool for degreasing the pan juices from a roast. There are dozens of models, most of them variations on the same design: a cup with a spout at its bottom that allows you to pour off the juices and leave the fat in the cup. With pitcher-type separators, there's always some fat in the spout that gets poured out with the juices.

We've found that the best model is one that allows the juices to drain from a hole in the bottom of the cup, which is opened by squeezing a lever in the handle.

Stock vs. broth: what's the difference

The art of stock and broth making is one of the first subjects you're taught in culinary school. Bones, you learn, are what make a stock a stock and not a broth. The bones, with little to no meat on them, lend gelatin to the stock, giving it "body." Stock may or may not also contain aromatics, like vegetables or herbs.

Broth, on the other hand, is made from meat, vegetables, and aromatics. Though it's sometimes made with meat still on the bone (as in broth made from a whole chicken, like the one below), broth's distinguishing flavor comes from the meat itself. Compared with stock, it has a lighter body and a more distinctly meaty (or vegetal) flavor.

Broth is more or less ready to eat, whereas stock typically needs some enhancement from additional ingredients or further cooking to turn it into something you'd want to eat. So if you're making a quick soup, broth is your best bet, but if it's a long-cooking soup, then either would work.

In a reduction sauce, stock may be the better option because it will produce a nice consistency without needing additional

thickeners. Reduced broth becomes very flavorful, but it lacks the body of reduced stock, and if the broth was highly seasoned to begin with, reduction may make it overly salty. This is especially true of commercially produced broths, which tend to be much saltier than homemade versions.

chicken broth

For the clearest broth, cook at the barest simmer and avoid stirring or agitating as much as possible.
Yields about 3 quarts

- 1 5- to 6-lb. chicken
- 1 lb. yellow onions (2 medium), peeled and cut into 2-inch pieces
- ½ lb. carrots (3 medium), peeled and cut into 2-inch pieces
- ¼ lb. celery (2 medium ribs), cut into 2-inch pieces
- 10 black peppercorns
- 3 large sprigs flat-leaf parsley
- 2 large sprigs thyme
- 1 bay leaf
- ¼ tsp. kosher salt; more to taste

If the giblets were included with the chicken, discard the liver and put the rest in a deep, narrow 8-quart stock pot. Remove the breast meat from the chicken and save for another use. Pull off and discard any large pieces of fat from the cavity opening.
Rinse the chicken, especially its cavity, and put it in the pot. Add 3 quarts cold water, plus more if necessary to cover the chicken. Bring to a simmer over medium-high heat and then reduce the heat to maintain a bare simmer. Cook for 30 minutes, skimming off any scum with a slotted spoon or skimmer.
Add the remaining ingredients, cover, and continue to cook at a bare simmer for 2 hours, adjusting the heat and skimming as necessary.

With tongs and a large slotted spoon or skimmer, remove most of the solids, transferring them to a bowl to cool before discarding. Slowly strain the broth through a fine sieve set over another large pot. If there are cloudy dregs as you near the bottom, stop straining and discard them.
Taste the broth; if you'd prefer its flavor to be more concentrated, simmer it until it's as flavorful as you like. Depending on how you'll be using the broth, you may want to season it with more salt at this point. If the broth is very fatty, chill it and then remove the solidified fat with a slotted spoon. Refrigerate for up to 5 days, or freeze for longer storage.

3 ways that salt helps roasting

Salt blocks bitterness

In addition to being a general flavor amplifier, salt has a special ability to enhance sweetness in foods. That's because sodium ions zero in on bitter flavor compounds and suppress them, making the sweet flavors seem stronger.

For the same reason, salt makes bitter foods more palatable. If you ever find that some of your roast's pan drippings have become too deeply browned (though not burned), don't despair. If you season it well you can still make a delicious pan sauce, because the salt will balance much of the bitterness.

Salt can make meat juicier

To guarantee your roast chicken turns out juicy, consider a brine.

Meats that tend to dry out during cooking—e.g., chicken, turkey, pork, shrimp—stay juicy and delicious if you brine them first. When you soak meat in brine, the salt water flows in, and the salt goes to work on the protein cells, altering them by loosening and unwinding the strands of protein and allowing them to sop up the brine. If you weigh your meat before and after brining, it will weigh more afterward, thanks to the liquid it has absorbed.

Of course, all this extra moisture would be useless if it were lost during cooking. But therein lies the magic of brining: The moisture isn't lost during cooking. Well, some is—that's inevitable because heat causes proteins to shrink and squeeze out liquid—but much less than if the meat hadn't been brined. The result is moister meat that's more flavorful, too, because the saltwater that the meat soaked up tastes good. For even better flavor, savvy chefs add other flavorings to their brine, like sugar, herbs, and spices; meat will drink in those flavors, too.

Salt tastes good—and makes everything else taste good

Why does salt taste good to us? According to the experts at the Monell Chemical Senses Center in Philadelphia, it boils down to biology. We like the taste because our bodies need sodium chloride.

And sprinkling a bit of sodium chloride onto other foods ensures that we'll consume lots of other essential nutrients, too, because salt makes pretty much everything else taste better. Thanks to its chemical nature, salt has the amazing ability to intensify agreeable tastes and diminish disagreeable ones. What more could a cook ask for?

Perhaps you've heard the old saw about salt bringing out the flavor of a dish. Well, the scientists at the Monell Center say it's absolutely true. The reason: Some flavor compounds are too subtle to detect, but when you add even just a teeny amount of salt, neurological magic happens: Suddenly, our taste receptors can detect flavors they weren't able to sense before.

So, when you add salt to roasted squash, the squash doesn't merely become salty; rather, the myriad complex flavors of the vegetable come to the fore.

Roasting pumpkin seeds

Roast the unhulled seeds you get from a whole pumpkin for use in the **Roasted Beet Salad with Crumbled Feta & Spicy Pepitas** on p. 10; they also make a great snack! Use your fingers to rake the seeds free from the strands of pumpkin fiber.

roasted pepitas

Yields 1 cup

- 1 **cup unhulled pepitas**
- 1 **Tbs. grapeseed oil**
- **Kosher salt**

Position a rack in the center of the oven and heat the oven to 400°F. In a small bowl, stir together the pepitas and grapeseed oil. Spread the seeds on a large baking sheet and sprinkle lightly with kosher salt. Roast until golden, 8 to 12 minutes. Cool and serve warm or at room temperature.

For spicy pepitas, sprinkle the seeds with chili powder, smoked paprika, curry powder, or another favorite spice before roasting. Or for a sweet treat, toss with cinnamon-sugar after roasting. Roasted pumpkin seeds will keep for several days stored in an airtight container at room temperature.

RECIPE	CALORIES (KCAL)	FAT CAL (KCAL)	PROTEIN (G)	CARB (G)	TOTAL FAT (G)	SAT FAT (G)	MONO FAT (G)	POLY FAT (G)	CHOL (MG)	SODIUM (MG)	FIBER (G)
SOUPS & SALADS, p. 4											
Roasted Potato and Mushroom Salad with Mascarpone	320	210	6	24	23	8	11	1.5	35	380	3
Roasted Hubbard Squash Soup with Hazelnuts and Chives	240	110	9	29	13	3	7	2	5	180	7
Cucumber, Fennel, and Potato Salad with Parsleyed Yogurt	210	100	6	22	11	4.5	6	1	10	270	4
Sweet Potato, Ham, and Goat Cheese Salad	520	350	24	19	39	11	23	3.5	60	1460	2
Southwest Tomato and Roasted Pepper Soup	170	110	5	11	12	4	7	1	10	220	3
Sweet Potato Soup w/Sorghum Butter & Duck Cracklings	370	240	7	27	27	14	10	1.5	70	380	3
Roasted Butternut Squash Salad with Pears and Stilton	560	310	18	50	35	12	15	2.5	60	1050	15
Roasted Beet Salad with Crumbled Feta & Spicy Pepitas	300	220	9	13	25	5	10	10	10	800	5
Roasted Chicken, Chickpea, and Cauliflower Salad	360	180	26	21	20	3.5	12	3.5	105	790	7
Roasted Potato Salad with Bell Peppers, Corn & Tomatoes	290	150	4	32	17	2.5	12	2	0	340	4
Roasted Broccoli and Farro Salad with Feta	280	140	10	29	15	4.5	8	1.5	15	660	6
VEGETABLES, p. 16											
Sweet Potato Oven Fries with Fry Sauce	120	70	2	12	7	1	2	4	5	370	2
Pan-Roasted Brussels Sprout Gratin w/Shallots	310	220	10	15	25	15	7	1	85	480	3
Roasted Sweet Potatoes w/Apples and Maple-Sage Butter	110	60	1	14	6	2.5	3	0	10	160	2
Roasted Garlic (per 1 Tbs.)	60	30	1	7	3.5	0	2.5	0	0	20	0
Pan-Roasted Sunchokes & Artichoke Hearts w/Herb Butter	160	80	3	17	9	3	4.5	.5	10	125	4
Roasted Fennel with Asiago and Thyme	150	80	5	12	10	2.5	6	1	10	250	5
Roasted Turnips with Maple and Cardamom	140	70	1	16	8	2.5	3	2.5	10	320	3
Pan-Roasted Carrots with Leeks, Pancetta, and Thyme	190	100	4	15	11	6	4	1	25	280	3
Roasted Brussels Sprouts with Wild Mushrooms and Cream	360	290	5	15	32	14	14	2	70	190	6
Honey-Roasted Radishes	90	25	1	16	3	2	1	0	10	210	3
Roasted Squash with Pimentón and Manchego Cheese	190	120	9	10	14	7	2.5	0.5	30	450	3
Roasted Root Vegetables with Meyer Lemon	190	80	2	26	10	1.5	710	1	0	280	8
Spicy Asian Roasted Broccoli and Snap Peas	290	180	7	24	20	3	11	5	0	800	6
FISH & SHELLFISH, p. 32											
Garlicky Shrimp with Basil	240	170	14	1	19	2.5	13	2	125	290	0
Miso-Roasted Atlantic Mackerel	520	320	38	9	36	7	15	10	120	330	0
Sear-Roasted Halibut with Blood Orange Salsa	380	160	37	18	18	2.5	11	2.5	55	510	3
Roasted Cod with Basil Pesto and Garlic Breadcrumbs	440	260	32	15	29	4	19	6	65	1200	3
Roasted Cod with Lemon-Parsley Crumbs	210	60	28	7	7	4	1.5	.5	80	410	0
Roasted Shrimp with Rosemary and Thyme	310	190	27	1	22	3	15	2.5	250	430	0
Salmon Fillets with Lemon-Rosemary Butter Sauce	440	270	37	2	30	13	11	4	140	600	0
Roasted Salmon and Asparagus with Lemon Oil	380	200	40	4	23	3.5	12	6	105	580	2
Spice-Rubbed, Sear-Roasted Salmon w/Glazed Fennel	430	220	40	14	24	3.5	13	6	105	960	4
Roasted Salmon with Mustard and Tarragon	350	180	39	1	20	3	6	9	110	500	0

The nutritional analyses have been calculated by a registered dietitian at Nutritional Solutions in Melville, New York. When a recipe gives a choice of ingredients, the first choice is the one used. Optional ingredients with measured amounts are included; ingredients without specific quantities are not. Analyses are per serving; when a range of ingredient amounts or servings is given, the smaller amount or portion is used. When the quantities of salt and pepper aren't specified, the analysis is based on ¼ tsp. salt and ⅛ tsp. pepper per serving for entrées, and ⅛ tsp. salt and ¹⁄₁₆ tsp. pepper per serving for side dishes.

RECIPE	CALORIES (KCAL)	FAT CAL (KCAL)	PROTEIN (G)	CARB (G)	TOTAL FAT (G)	SAT FAT (G)	MONO FAT (G)	POLY FAT (G)	CHOL (MG)	SODIUM (MG)	FIBER (G)
POULTRY, p. 46											
Rosemary-Garlic Chicken with Apple and Fig Compote	420	150	32	34	17	3	6	6	80	950	3
Roasted Cornish Game Hens with Cranberry-Port Sauce	490	290	36	9	32	10	14	6	210	960	1
Lemon-Garlic Roast Chicken with Yuzu Kosho	370	120	58	0	14	2.5	7	3.5	160	370	1
Roast Chicken with Fingerling Potatoes, Leeks, and Bacon	760	340	61	43	38	12	15	7	190	1220	5
Turkey Thighs w/Porcini, Sausage & Artichoke Hearts	270	160	19	8	17	4	8	2.5	105	640	2
Pan-Roasted Chicken with Olives and Lemon	630	360	60	6	40	11	18	7	200	850	1
Roasted Turkey Breast, Porchetta-Style	480	230	56	1	26	7	11	4.5	155	960	0
Butter-and-Herb-Roasted Turkey with Madeira Jus	440	210	47	3	24	8	9	4.5	145	490	0
Plum-Glazed Duck Breasts	300	100	24	27	11	3	5	1.5	135	500	0
Fresh Herb- and Salt-Rubbed Roasted Turkey	510	220	68	0	24	7	8	6	200	1500	0
Roast Chicken Breasts w/Rosemary-Lemon Brown Butter	360	210	35	1	24	10	8	4	130	360	0
Maple-Glazed Roast Chicken	550	230	52	26	26	7	10	6	165	1290	0
Roast Chicken with Chanterelles and Peas	970	630	57	22	70	30	27	8	280	430	6
Mediterranean Chicken with Mushrooms & Zucchini	470	240	43	10	27	7	12	5	135	590	2
Pomegranate-Orange Chicken	650	340	45	35	37	7	12	15	125	300	6
Chicken with Apples & Cider	480	230	41	18	25	9	9	4.5	140	480	4
Citrus-Marinated Roasted Chicken	390	220	40	3	24	6	1	5	125	360	0
Roasted Duck with Tangerine-Hoisin Glaze	820	590	44	9	66	22	30	9	190	1070	1
Roasted Goose w/Prune Stuffing and Red-Wine Gravy	940	530	68	28	59	18	27	7	235	780	3
Regionally Inspired Roast Turkey	460	180	64	0	21	7	7	5	255	410	0
New England Turkey Gravy (per ¼ cup)	80	40	3	7	4.5	2	2	0	10	210	0
Southern Turkey Gravy (per ¼ cup)	90	40	3	5	4.5	2	2	0	10	200	0
Southwest Turkey Gravy (per ¼ cup)	100	40	3	7	4.5	2	2	0	10	200	0
California Turkey Gravy (per ¼ cup)	120	40	3	8	4.5	2	2	0	10	210	0
Pacific NW Turkey Gravy (per ¼ cup)	100	40	4	6	4.5	2	2	0	10	210	1
Midwest Turkey Gravy (per ¼ cup)	100	60	3	5	7	3.5	3	0	20	250	0
BEEF & LAMB, p. 76											
Sear-Roasted Sirloin Tip Steaks (w/1 Tbs. butter)	350	200	35	1	22	8	10	1.5	100	470	0
Roasted Lamb Loins with Mustard-Herb Crust	240	120	21	7	13	3.5	8	1	65	420	1
Pesto-Crusted Racks of Lamb	300	210	18	2	24	8	12	2.5	65	180	0
Hanger Steak with Spicy Miso Glaze	460	200	43	12	22	7	9	5	130	570	0
Vietnamese-Style Lamb Riblets w/Soy Dipping Sauce	340	220	19	11	25	9	10	3	75	1710	1
Spice-Rubbed Roast Beef Tenderloin with Red-Wine Sauce	570	310	45	4	35	13	15	1.5	165	470	1
Slow-Roasted Leg of Lamb with Mint and Lemon	710	270	97	3	30	9	15	2.5	295	520	0
Beef Tenderloin with Roquefort-Pecan Butter	640	470	39	3	53	21	21	6	170	730	1
Rosemary-Garlic Roast Leg of Lamb with Red Potatoes	370	130	40	19	14	4	8	1	115	530	2
Slow-Roasted Standing Rib Roast w/Brown Ale Butter Sauce	720	350	78	4	40	17	16	1.5	195	520	1

continued on p. 144

RECIPE	CALORIES (KCAL)	FAT CAL (KCAL)	PROTEIN (G)	CARB (G)	TOTAL FAT (G)	SAT FAT (G)	MONO FAT (G)	POLY FAT (G)	CHOL (MG)	SODIUM (MG)	FIBER (G)
PORK, p. 92											
Fresh Ham with Rosemary, Garlic, and Lemon	760	490	57	4	54	21	26	4.5	215	680	0
Pernil-Style Pork Tenderloin	330	180	31	5	20	4	13	2	95	290	1
Pork Chops with Cider-Dijon Pan Sauce	290	130	27	12	15	7	5	1	85	440	1
Tuscan-Style Roast Pork with Rosemary, Sage, and Garlic	290	140	32	2	16	4.5	9	1	85	1010	0
Pork Crown Roast with Stuffing and Brandy Cream Sauce	1220	420	106	69	47	19	19	6	300	830	6
Pork Tenderloin with Pears and Cider	360	160	28	23	18	9	7	1	100	380	3
Tuscan Roast Pork w/Potatoes, Fennel, and Parsnips	600	200	49	44	23	5	13	2	110	1070	7
Glazed Pork Loin with Pineapple-Scallion Chutney	290	90	32	18	9	3	5	.5	80	470	1
Pork Chops Stuffed with Pine Nuts and Herbs	440	300	25	11	33	7	15	8	65	230	1
Slow-Roasted Pork Shoulder w/Carrots, Onions, and Garlic	630	260	75	6	29	11	13	3.5	235	1090	1
Roast Pork with Crisp Crackling and Red Currant Gravy	850	490	71	12	55	24	21	4	255	760	1
LEFTOVERS, p. 108											
Moussaka Gratinée	400	220	27	14	25	9	12	2	125	1020	4
Lamb Niçoise Salad with Potatoes and Fava Beans	620	350	33	35	39	7	26	4.5	130	1330	6
Turkey Bolognese	420	210	32	12	23	8	9	3.5	100	1980	1
Turkey Soup with Dill, Parsley, and Chive Dumplings	530	230	27	44	26	11	10	3	180	1360	7
Ham Lo Mein with Shiitake and Snow Peas	580	210	27	65	24	5	10	6	110	1410	5
Pulled-Pork Sandwiches w/Cabbage, Caper, and Herb Slaw	360	180	28	12	20	5	12	2.5	80	720	2
Turkey Noodle Casserole	500	210	28	43	24	11	9	2.5	100	760	2
Indian Lamb Curry with Green Beans and Cashews	530	220	40	41	24	8	11	2.5	110	800	6
Pork Ragoût with Soft Polenta	550	240	35	44	27	10	12	3	95	1090	5
Pork and Potato Hash with Poached Eggs and Avocado	510	230	27	43	26	6	15	3	265	910	8
DESSERTS, p. 120											
Roasted Strawberry Shortcakes with Vanilla Biscuits	509	231	6	63	26	16	6	1	95	331	3
Roasted Strawberries	143	4	1	36	0	0	0	0	0	1	3
Roasted Plantains with Brown Sugar and Rum	50	25	0	7	2.5	0	1.5	1	0	480	1
Roasted Rhubarb Granita	120	5	2	29	0	0	0	0	0	20	3
Sugar-Roasted Peaches	60	20	1	10	2.5	1	1	0	0	10	1
Sugar-Roasted Peach & Cornbread Sundaes w/Syrup	620	230	9	91	26	14	8	2	130	280	3
Roasted Red Grapes with Mascarpone and Rum	370	250	5	28	27	14	8	1	70	330	1
TEST KITCHEN, p. 128											
Herb Gravy for a Brined Turkey (per ¼ cup)	60	25	7	3	2.5	0	1.5	0	15	230	0
Red-Wine Chicken Stock (per ½ cup)	90	15	4	5	2	1	0.5	0	0	430	0
Yorkshire Pudding	240	130	6	21	14	6	6	1.5	85	170	1

METRIC EQUIVALENTS

LIQUID/DRY MEASURES

U.S.	METRIC
¼ teaspoon	1.25 milliliters
½ teaspoon	2.5 milliliters
1 teaspoon	5 milliliters
1 tablespoon (3 teaspoons)	15 milliliters
1 fluid ounce (2 tablespoons)	30 milliliters
¼ cup	60 milliliters
⅓ cup	80 milliliters
½ cup	120 milliliters
1 cup	240 milliliters
1 pint (2 cups)	480 milliliters
1 quart (4 cups; 32 ounces)	960 milliliters
1 gallon (4 quarts)	3.84 liters
1 ounce (by weight)	28 grams
1 pound	454 grams
2.2 pounds	1 kilogram

OVEN TEMPERATURES

°F	GAS MARK	°C
250	½	120
275	1	140
300	2	150
325	3	165
350	4	180
375	5	190
400	6	200
425	7	220
450	8	230
475	9	240
500	10	260
550	Broil	290

Bruce Aidells is America's go-to expert for all matters involving meat and meat cookery. He has a national cooking show called Good Cookin' with Bruce Aidells on the cable network Live Well. He also writes recipe articles for *Bon Appétit* magazine, *Real Food* magazine, and *Fine Cooking* and is a contributing editor to *Eating Well* magazine. His latest cookbook is *The Great Meat Cookbook*.
- Turkey Thighs Stuffed with Porcini, Sausage, and Artichoke Hearts, FC#107
- Roasted Turkey Breast, Porchetta-Style, FC#107

Jennifer Armentrout is chief editor at *Fine Cooking* magazine.
- Basic Roasted Green Beans, FC#88
- Roasted Sweet Potatoes with Apples and Maple-Sage Butter, FC#113
- Pan-Roasted Sunchokes and Artichoke Hearts with Lemon-Herb Butter, FC#103

When she's not cooking for her family, **Julie Grimes Bottcher** writes about food and develops recipes in Birmingham, Alabama.
- Spicy Asian Roasted Broccoli and Snap Peas, FC#70

Ronne Day, associate food editor/stylist at *Fine Cooking,* was classically trained at the French Culinary Institute and received her MFA from New York University.
- Roast Chicken with Chanterelles and Peas, FC#125
- Roasted Root Vegetables with Meyer Lemon, FC#120

Fine Cooking contributing editor **Tasha DeSerio** is a chef, caterer, and author of *Salad for Dinner.*
- Roasted Broccoli and Farro Salad with Feta, FC#107
- Roasted Brussels Sprouts with Wild Mushrooms and Cream, FC#107
- Slow-Roasted Pork Shoulder with Carrots, Onions, and Garlic, FC#97
- Pulled-Pork Sandwiches with Cabbage, Caper, and Herb Slaw, FC#97
- Pork Ragoût with Soft Polenta, FC#97
- Pork and Potato Hash with Poached Eggs and Avocado, FC#97

Paula Disbrowe is the editor in chief at *Tribeza* magazine. Formerly the chef at Hart & Hind Ranch in Texas, she is also the author of *Cowgirl Cuisine.*
- Roasted Beet Salad with Crumbled Feta and Spicy Pepitas, FC#70

Tom Douglas is a chef, restaurateur, and writer, with five Seattle restaurants and a James Beard Award for Best Northwest Chef in 1994. He has written four cookbooks, the latest of which is *The Dahlia Bakery Cookbook.*
- Spice-Rubbed, Sear-Roasted Salmon with Maple Glazed Fennel, FC#92

Fine Cooking contributing editor **Allison Ehri Kreitler** lives in Milford, Connecticut, where she juggles food styling, writing, cooking instruction, and being a mom.
- Rosemary-Garlic Chicken with Apple and Fig Compote, FC#95

Dividing her time between Provence and Minneapolis, **Mary Ellen Evans** leads gastronomic tours of France and has written two chicken cookbooks.
- Mediterranean Chicken with Mushrooms and Zucchini, FC#91
- Pomegranate-Orange Chicken, FC#91
- Chicken with Apples and Cider, FC#91

Melissa Gaman is a freelance recipe developer, editor, and writer who blogs at Cookies to Couscous.
- Pork Chops with Cider-Dijon Pan Sauce, FC#115

Honolulu-based food writer, cookbook author, and recipe developer **Dabney Gough** has published two cookbooks, *Bi-Rite Market's Eat Good Food* and *Sweet Cream and Sugar Cones.* Dabney is also a former *Fine Cooking* editor.
- Glazed Pork Loin with Pineapple-Scallion Chutney, FC#115

Trine Hahnemann has written five cookbooks in her native Danish and two in English, including *Scandinavian Christmas.* She started out as a caterer for rock stars and today owns and runs a café in Denmark's House of Parliament as well as several large corporate cafés. Trine also writes for zesterdaily.com and appears regularly in magazines and newspapers in the United States, Britain, and Denmark. She lives in Copenhagen.
- Roast Pork with Crisp Crackling & Red Currant Gravy, FC#126
- Red-Wine Chicken Stock, FC#126

Martha Holmberg is an award-winning magazine editor, Paris-trained chef, and Portland, Oregon–based cookbook author. Her latest book is *Fresh Food Nation.*
- Sweet Potato Oven Fries with Fry Sauce, FC#114

Linton Hopkins is executive chef and owner of Restaurant Eugene and Holeman & Finch Public House in Atlanta. He also works with Delta airlines on Business Elite® menus for flights between Atlanta and Europe. Linton was named the 2012 James Beard Best Chef Southeast.
- Roasted Sweet Potato Soup with Sorghum Butter and Duck Cracklings, FineCooking.com

Arlene Jacobs has cooked at some of New York's finest restaurants and has been an instructor at her alma mater, The French Culinary Institute. Now, she's a freelance food writer, recipe developer, and food stylist.
- Roast Chicken with Fingerling Potatoes, Leeks, and Bacon, FC#116
- Roast Chicken Breasts with Rosemary-Lemon Brown Butter, FC#127
- Hanger Steak with Spicy Miso Glaze, FC#116
- Rosemary-Garlic Roast Leg of Lamb with Red Potatoes, FC#116
- Pernil-Style Pork Tenderloin, FC#121
- Tuscan Roast Pork with Yellow Potatoes, Fennel, and Parsnips, FC#116

Cookbook author and food writer **Jeanne Kelley** has written four books, including the *Kitchen Garden Cookbook* and *Blue Eggs and Yellow Tomatoes*. She lives in Los Angeles, where she raises chickens and bees.
- Citrus-Marinated Roasted Chicken, FC#115
- Regionally Inspired Roast Turkey, FC#125
- Regionally Inspired Roast Turkey Gravies, FC#125

Lori Longbotham is a recipe developer and cookbook author whose books include *Luscious Coconut Desserts* and *Luscious Creamy Desserts*. She is formerly food editor at *Gourmet*.
- Roasted Strawberry Shortcakes with Vanilla Biscuits, FC#72
- Roasted Strawberries, FC#72

James Beard Award–winner **Barbara Lynch** is regarded as one of Boston's—and the country's—leading chefs and restaurateurs and is the author of *Stir: Mixing It Up in the Italian Tradition*. She established the Barbara Lynch Foundation in 2012, a charitable organization that is dedicated to, among other things, improving access to nutritious foods.
- Cucumber, Fennel, and Roasted Potato Salad with Parsleyed Yogurt, FC#92

Ivy Manning is a Portland, Oregon-based freelance food and travel writer, food stylist, and author of *Crackers & Dips, The Adaptable Feast, The Farm to Table Book,* and *Better from Scratch*.
- Roasted Hubbard Squash Soup with Hazelnuts and Chives, FC#95

Diane Posner Mastro is former chef-owner of Enoteca. She is now involved in education and animal-welfare projects.
- Roasted Rhubarb Granita, FC#2

Jennifer McLagan has worked as a chef in Australia, England, and Canada. She has participated at the Food & Wine Classic in Aspen, the Melbourne Food & Wine Festival Master Class Series, and the Epicurean Classic in Michigan. She is a regular contributor to food magazines and is the author of four books: *Cooking on the Bone, Bones, Fat,* and *Odd Bits: How to Cook the Rest of the Animal*.
- Garlicky Shrimp with Basil, FC#92
- Slow-Roasted Leg of Lamb with Mint and Lemon, FC#104
- Moussaka Gratinée; Lamb Niçoise Salad with Potatoes and Fava Beans, FC#104
- Indian Lamb Curry with Green Beans and Cashews, FC#104

Scott Megill is chef de cuisine at Talula's Daily, a gourmet market and café in Philadelphia. Before that, the Philly native spent time in Napa Valley attending the Culinary Institute of America and cooked at Equinox in Washington, D.C.
- Maple-Glazed Roast Chicken, FC#127

Perla Meyers is the award-winning author of six cookbooks, including *The Peasant Kitchen* and *Perla Meyers' Art of Seasonal Cooking*. She attended the Ecole Hoteliere in Switzerland, studied baking and confection at the Hotel Sacher in Vienna, and received a degree from Le Cordon Bleu in Paris. Meyers conducts cooking workshops throughout the United States and Canada.
- Southwest Tomato and Roasted Pepper Soup, FC#91

Susie Middleton is editor at large at *Fine Cooking*. She cooks, writes, and farms on her Green Island Farm on Martha's Vineyard. Her newest book is *Fresh from the Farm: A Year of Recipes and Stories*.
- Roasted Turnips with Maple and Cardamom, FC#101
- Pan-Roasted Carrots with Leeks, Pancetta, and Thyme, FC#116

Diane Morgan is an award-winning cookbook author, freelance food writer, culinary instructor, and restaurant consultant based in Portland, Oregon. She is the author of 17 cookbooks, including *Roots*.
- Honey-Roasted Radishes, FC#122

David Myers is an award-winning chef and restaurateur with a career spanning two decades. His latest restaurant venture is Hinoki & the Bird. David also starred in the TV show Shopping with Chefs on the Fine Living channel.
- Lemon-Garlic Roast Chicken with Yuzu Kosho, FC#120

Artisan baker **David Norman** is the head baker and partner at Easy Tiger in Austin, Texas.
- Roasted Beet Salad with Crumbled Feta and Spicy Pepitas, David Norman, FC#70

After a long stint in New York City, where she was the test kitchen director for *Saveur*, **Liz Pearson** returned to her native Texas, where she writes about food for many publications and websites.
- Roasted Potato and Mushroom Salad with Mascarpone, FC#97
- Roasted Red Grapes with Mascarpone and Rum, FC#107

Fine Cooking contributing editor **Melissa Pellegrino** is co-author with her husband of *The Italian Farmer's Table* and *The Southern Italian Farmer's Table*. The couple owns Bufalina Wood Fired Pizza in Guilford, Connecticut.
- Roasted Chicken, Chickpea, and Cauliflower Salad, FC#126
- Pan-Roasted Chicken with Olives and Lemon, FC#103

Recipe developer and food writer **Laraine Perri** has published nearly 500 recipes in more than a dozen national publications.
- Roasted Fennel with Asiago and Thyme, FC#113
- Roasted Salmon with Mustard and Tarragon, FC#122
- Pork Tenderloin with Pears and Cider, FC#125

Joanna Pruess is the award-winning author of 10 cookbooks, including *Seduced by Bacon*. A world traveler, she also teaches cooking classes and speaks regularly about food and cultural anthropology.
- Plum-Glazed Duck Breasts, FC#114

Julissa Roberts is test kitchen manager and assistant food editor at *Fine Cooking* magazine.
- Pan-Roasted Brussels Sprout Gratin with Shallots and Rosemary, FC#113

Fine Cooking contributing editor **Tony Rosenfeld** is executive chef and co-owner of b.good, a Boston-based restaurant chain. He also is a cookbook author and food writer.
- Sweet Potato, Ham, and Goat Cheese Salad, FC#102
- Roasted Butternut Squash Salad with Pears and Stilton, FC#120
- Roasted Cod with Basil Pesto and Garlic Breadcrumbs; Basil Pesto, FC#66
- Salmon Fillets with Lemon-Rosemary Butter Sauce, FC#71
- Roasted Salmon with Asparagus and Lemon Oil, FC#77
- Sear-Roasted Sirloin Tip Steaks with Café de Paris Butter, FC#123

Mark Scarbrough and **Bruce Weinstein** have written more than 20 cookbooks, including *The Ultimate Frozen Dessert Book*, *The Ultimate Ice Cream Book*, and their most recent, *The Great American Slow Cooker Book*. They also pen the column "Sundays in the Kitchen with Bruce and Mark" on weightwatchers.com.
- Roasted Shrimp with Rosemary and Thyme, FC#110
- Pesto-Crusted Racks of Lamb, FC#120
- Slow-Roasted Beef Standing Rib Roast with Brown Ale Butter Sauce, FC#120
- Fresh Ham with Rosemary, Garlic, and Lemon, FC#108
- Pork Crown Roast with Dried-Fruit-Sourdough Stuffing and Brandy Cream Sauce, FC#120
- Ham Lo Mein with Shiitake and Snow Peas, FC#108

Samantha Seneviratne is a former associate food editor and food stylist at *Fine Cooking*.
- Roasted Garlic, FC#104
- Pork Chops Stuffed with Pine Nuts and Herbs, FC#110

Tania Sigal is chef of Tania's Table in North Miami Beach, Florida, as well as a cooking instructor.
- Roasted Plantains with Brown Sugar and Rum, FC#56

Maria Helm Sinskey is the culinary director of Robert Sinskey Vineyards in Napa Valley, which she owns with her husband.
- Roasted Squash with Pimentón and Manchego Cheese, FC#117
- Fresh Herb- and Salt-Rubbed Roasted Turkey, FC#107
- Turkey Bolognese, FC#107
- Turkey Soup with Dill, Parsley, and Chive Dumplings, FC#107
- Turkey Noodle Casserole, FC#107
- Herb Gravy for a Brined Turkey, FC#107

Melissa Speck works with her husband Paul at the Speck family winery—Henry of Pelham Family Estate Winery—in St. Catharines, Ontario, Canada.
- Tuscan-Style Roast Pork with Rosemary, Sage, and Garlic, FC#101

Fine Cooking contributing editor **Molly Stevens** is a food writer, cookbook author, editor, and cooking teacher. Her cookbook *All About Roasting* won a 2012 James Beard Foundation Award and two IACP awards.

- Roasted Cod with Lemon-Parsley Crumbs, FC#89
- Roasted Cornish Game Hens with Cranberry-Port Sauce, FC#102
- Roasted Duck with Tangerine-Hoisin Glaze, FC#102
- Roasted Goose with Prune Stuffing and Red-Wine Gravy, FC#102
- Roasted Lamb Loins with Mustard-Herb Crust, FC#110
- Vietnamese-Style Lamb Riblets with Sweet Soy Dipping Sauce, FC#110
- Spice-Rubbed Roast Beef Tenderloin with Red-Wine Sauce, FC#114

Bill Taibe is the chef/owner of LeFarm and The Whelk restaurants, both in Westport, Connecticut. He's a leader of the local-food movement in that state.

- Sugar-Roasted Peaches, FC#118
- Sugar-Roasted Peach and Sundaes with Bacon Syrup, FC#118

James Beard–award winning author **Anna Thomas** has written several books, including *The Vegetarian Epicure Books 1 and 2, The New Vegetarian Epicure,* and *Love Soup.* She also is an Academy Award–nominated filmmaker and screenwriter.

- Butter-and-Herb-Roasted Turkey with Madeira Jus, FC#113

Jay Weinstein is a New York City-based food writer and former chef. His latest book is *The Ethical Gourmet.*

- Miso-Roasted Atlantic Mackerel, FC#101

Joanne Weir is a cooking teacher, chef, cookbook author, and television host. Her first restaurant, Copita, opened in Sausalito, California, in 2013. Her latest book is *Joanne Weir's Cooking Confidence,* the companion book to her television show of the same name.

- Roasted Potato Salad with Bell Peppers, FC#80
- Sear-Roasted Halibut with Blood Orange Salsa, FC#97

Shelley Wiseman was the senior food editor of *Fine Cooking.* A former food editor at *Gourmet* and the author of *Just Tacos,* she lived for many years in Mexico, where she ran her own cooking school specializing in French cuisine.

- Beef Tenderloin with Roquefort-Pecan Butter, FC#119
- Yorkshire Pudding, FC#120

INDEX

If you like this book, you'll love *Fine Cooking*.

Read *Fine Cooking* Magazine:

Get six idea-filled issues including FREE digital access. Every issue is packed with triple-tested recipes, expert advice, step-by-step techniques – everything for people who love to cook!

Subscribe today at:
FineCooking.com/4Sub

Discover our *Fine Cooking* Online Store:

It's your destination for premium resources from America's best cookbook writers, chefs, and bakers: cookbooks, DVDs, videos, special interest publications, and more.

Visit today at:
FineCooking.com/4More

Get our FREE *Fine Cooking* eNewsletter:

Our *Make It Tonight* weekday email supplies you with no-fail recipes for quick, wholesome meals; our weekly eNewsletter inspires with seasonal recipes, holiday menus, and more.

Sign up, it's free:
FineCooking.com/4Newsletter

Become a CooksClub member

Join to enjoy unlimited online access to member-only content and exclusive benefits, including: recipes, menus, techniques, and videos; our Test Kitchen Hotline; digital issues; monthly giveaways, contests, and special offers.

Discover more information online:
FineCooking.com/4Join